NL
1850

Jérôme Brunet | Eric Saunier

Sebastian Redecke

Jérôme Brunet | Eric Saunier
Urban Sites | Urbane Orte

Birkhäuser – Publishers for Architecture
Birkhäuser – Verlag für Architektur
Basel · Berlin · Boston

Translation German/English and French/English:
Susanne Schindler

Layout and cover design:
Schack Verlagsherstellung/Ulrike Schöber

A CIP catalogue record for this book is available
from the Library of Congress, Washington, D.C.,
USA

Deutsche Bibliothek Cataloging-in-Publication Data

[Jérôme Brunet, Eric Saunier, urban sites] Jérôme
Brunet, Eric Saunier, urban sites, urbane Orte /
Sebastian Redecke. [Transl. German/Engl.: Susanne
Schindler]. – Basel ; Berlin ; Boston : Birkhäuser,
2001

ISBN 3-7643-6173-5

© 2001 Birkhäuser – Publishers for Architecture,
P.O.Box 133, CH-4010 Basel, Switzerland
A member of the BertelsmannSpringer Publishing
Group

Printed on acid-free paper produced from
chlorine-free pulp. TCF ∞

Printed in Germany

ISBN 3-7643-6173-5

http://www.birkhauser.ch

9 8 7 6 5 4 3 2 1

Contents

Inhalt

Nîmes has its magnificent Roman amphitheatre. The oval structure, erected in the first century AD in Flavian times, is a notable 133 metres long and 101 metres wide. Its facades are characterised by the typical rhythm of massive rows of arcades, the lower row ordered by pilasters, the upper by engaged Doric columns. The best-preserved Roman theatre, with its 7000 seats and a new, spectacular roof by Labfac architects, is used today for large-scale events ranging from a night of opera to a tennis tournament. To the north and west, the building becomes a part of the old town with its tightly packed houses. Narrow streets unexpectedly open onto the Boulevard des Arènes that circles the big round in the north. The only exception in the dense urban tissue is the wide Boulevard Victor Hugo. It leads north to another building of antiquity, the Maison Carrée, a well-preserved podium temple, and to

Encounters | Die Begegnung

Nîmes hat sein prachtvolles römisches Amphitheater. Es handelt sich um einen im ersten Jahrhundert nach Christus, in flavischer Zeit, errichteten ovalen Bau mit einer beachtlichen Länge von 133 Metern und einer Breite von 101 Metern. Die Fassaden werden vom typischen Rhythmus einer mächtigen Arkadenreihe bestimmt, wobei die untere Reihe durch Pilaster, die obere durch dorische Wandsäulen gegliedert ist. Das besterhaltene römische Theater mit seinen 7000 Zuschauerplätzen und neuer, spektakulärer Arenenüberdachung von dem Büro Labfac wird heute für Großveranstaltungen vom Opernabend bis zum Tennisturnier genutzt. Nördlich und westlich ist der Bau in die Altstadt mit ihren dichtgedrängten Häusern eingebunden. Enge Gassen öffnen sich unvermittelt auf den Boulevard des Arènes, der das große Rund nördlich umgreift. Eine Ausnahme im engen städtischen Gefüge bildet nur der breite Boulevard Victor Hugo, der nach Norden führt – zum ebenfalls antiken Maison Carrée, einem gut erhaltenen Podientempel, und zur Carré d'Art, dem Kultur-

Facade detail of the elementary school "de la Placette" in Nîmes

Fassadendetail der Grundschule „de la Placette" in Nîmes

the Carré d'Art, the city's cultural centre designed by Norman Foster. The change from the density of the old town to the expanse of the large square with the amphitheatre is striking. Seen from different directions it is surprising again and again.

Only 250 metres to the west of the theatre there is a totally different situation. Upon entering Rue de l'Hôtel-Dieu behind Clinique Saint-Joseph, one steps onto the small Place de l'Oratoire, a triangular square in one of the most beautiful parts of the old town. On its northern edge, the square is bordered by a long, very technical looking facade of aluminium slats. This is the first, to begin with puzzling encounter with the architecture of Jérôme Brunet and Eric Saunier.

This facade speaks their architectural language on several levels. In an exemplary way, it demonstrates how Brunet and Saunier tackle a design problem. First of all, it is characteristic that the architects do not hesitate to develop a fundamentally new and innovative facade structure. Upon closer inspection, however, it also becomes clear that they nevertheless succeed in integrating the building into its surround-

bau der Stadt von Norman Foster. Der Wechsel von der Enge zur Weite des großflächigen Platzes mit dem Amphitheater ist spannungsreich und aus verschiedenen Blickwinkeln betrachtet immer wieder überraschend.

Folgt man dem Weg an dem Theater vorbei weiter nach Westen, so zeigt sich nach nur 250 Metern ein anderes Bild. Nachdem man hinter der Clinique Saint-Joseph in die Rue de l'Hôtel-Dieu eingebogen ist, erblickt man inmitten eines der schönsten Teile der Altstadt die kleine dreieckige Place de l'Oratoire, die im Norden von einer langgezogenen, sehr technisch wirkenden Fassade aus Aluminiumlamellen abgeschlossen wird. Es ist dies die erste, zunächst irritierende Begegnung mit der Architektur von Jérôme Brunet und Eric Saunier.

Diese Fassade spricht in mehrfacher Hinsicht ihre Architektursprache. Sie zeigt exemplarisch, wie sie eine Entwurfsaufgabe in die Hand nehmen. Es ist für die Architekten zunächst charakteristisch, daß sie sich nicht scheuen, grundlegend eine neue, innovative Struktur einer Fassade zu erarbeiten. Bei näherer Betrachtung wird außerdem deutlich, daß es ihnen dennoch gelingt, sich in das Ensemble der Umge-

ing ensemble, in this case the historic fabric and the adjoining church, Temple de l'Oratoire. Brunet and Saunier took the brief for the new building and the redesign of the Place de l'Oratoire to be one task demanding a harmonious balancing-act. With great resoluteness in design they created a four-storey school building for 500 pupils, establishing a new visual focus in the neighbourhood. Completed in 1991, the Ecole de la Placette comprises a building from the early 1900s and a new building. The architects simply "doubled" the old building volume on its south side. Old and new are engaged in an intense dialogue best experienced in the central corridors. Here the interior walls, with doors to the classrooms of both building parts, stand face to face.

Their resoluteness in design, however, is most apparent in the new facade facing the square. Up to the parapet of the open roofstorey, the facade is one continuous, long front made up of simple aluminium slats grouped into panels, a delicate structure producing an ever-changing play of shadows. The architects think of it as a "transcription of a greatly enlarged Venetian blind". Each framed panel with its

bung – hier die Altbauten mit der unmittelbar angrenzenden Kirche de l'Oratoire – einzufügen. Brunet und Saunier haben die Bauaufgabe und die Neugestaltung der Place de l'Oratoire als Einheit begriffen, die nach einem harmonischen Ausgleich verlangt. Mit großer entwerferischer Entschiedenheit ist hier ein viergeschossiger Schulbau für rund 500 Kinder entstanden, der visuell einen neuen Mittelpunkt des Quartiers bildet. Die Ende 1991 fertiggestellte Ecole de la Placette setzt sich aus einem Altbau aus dem Anfang des letzten Jahrhunderts und einem Neubau zusammen. Die Architekten haben den alten Gebäuderiegel nach Süden einfach nur „aufgedoppelt". Alt und Neu stehen in einem spannungsvollen Dialog miteinander, der vor allem im zentralen Flurbereich erlebt werden kann, wo die internen Wände mit den Klassentüren von beiden Hausteilen einander gegenüberstehen.

Die entwerferische Entschiedenheit zeigt sich jedoch in erster Linie nicht hier, sondern vor allem in der neuen Fassade zum Platz. Es handelt sich durchgehend, bis zur Brüstung des offenen Dachgeschosses, um eine lange Front schlichter Aluminiumlamellen, die, in einzelne Felder gefügt, eine feingliedrige Struktur mit immer wieder anderen Schattenspielen bilden. Von den Architekten wird die Fassa-

fixed slats – except those at the level of the parapets or in front of a closed wall surface – can be pivoted around a central axis. The unobstructed view of the square is therefore available to all.

Fundamental considerations of context constitute a further theme in the architects' work. Unwilling to be categorised by building type or vocabulary, this is taking a risky position. They are not interested in searching for the easy, perhaps obvious path. They want to transform a place architecturally, want to redefine it. With their daring attitude, it is astonishing that ever since they founded their practice in 1981, Jérôme Brunet and Eric Saunier were awarded almost all commissions as the result of architectural competitions. In these competitions, time and again they presented unconventional, newly developed facades. With great dedication, they managed to present their concepts in a vivid and convincing way.

In the competition for Nîmes, they chose to clad the new building's southern front with an aluminium structure to counteract the extreme overheating of the building

de als „Transkription einer gewaltig vergrößerten Jalousie" gesehen. Jedes der gerahmten Elemente mit den fest fixierten Lamellen läßt sich – soweit es nicht in der Brüstungsebene oder vor einer geschlossenen Wandzone angebracht wurde – um eine vertikale Mittelachse drehen. Der freie Ausblick auf den Platz ist somit jedem gewährt.

Es ist die grundlegende Überlegung zum Ort, die sich bei der Arbeit der Architekten weitergehend interpretieren läßt. Sie lassen es sich nicht aufzwingen, sich einem Bautypus oder Vokabular unterzuordnen, und riskieren damit viel. Sie suchen nicht den einfachen, zunächst naheliegenden Weg, sondern wollen einen Raum architektonisch verwandeln, neu bestimmen. Es verwundert daher, daß Jérôme Brunet und Eric Saunier seit 1981, als sie ihr gemeinsames Büro gegründet haben, mit ihrer mutigen Haltung fast alle ihre Aufträge über Wettbewerbe erhielten. Immer wieder mit anderen Konzepten haben sie bei diesen Wettbewerben neu entwickelte Fassaden vorgestellt, die vom Vertrauten abweichen. Es gelang ihnen dabei mit großem Engagement, ihre Konzepte bildhaft zu präsentieren und damit zu überzeugen.

in summer. The aluminium slat wall was set in front of the actual, mostly glazed facade in a way that seems self-explanatory to the architects. Because only simple building materials were used in this double facade, construction costs did not exceed the budget. In addition, the building's certain hermetic quality that results when the slat wall is closed prevents pupils from being too distracted by gazing out or being seen.

It would surely have been too provocative to extend the uncompromising aluminium skin across the entire length of the building. It was therefore ingeniously "played down" by other elements. A sunken playground for the first graders is open to the square in front of the building. By placing it there, an additional floor was gained, passers-by have a view of this partially planted open area, and the younger children can play in a space that is outdoors, but separated from the street.

Another measure to reduce the dominance of the aluminium slats is a part of the facade itself. On the second and third floors, two large, loggia-like openings are

In Nîmes entschieden sie sich beim Wettbewerb, die Südseite des neuen Gebäuderiegels mit der vorgestellten Aluminiumkonstruktion zu gestalten, um der extremen Aufheizung im Sommer entgegenzutreten. Die Aluminiumlamellen-Wand wurde so vor die eigentliche, größtenteils verglaste Fassade gestellt, daß sie sich nach Auffassung der Architekten ohne Erläuterungen selbst erklärt. Es ergab sich zudem, daß mit dieser doppelten Fassade aus einfachsten Elementen die Kosten im Rahmen blieben. Mit der gewissen Abschottung bei geschlossener Lamellen-Wand ist außerdem dafür gesorgt, daß die Schüler durch direkte Aus- und Einblicke nicht abgelenkt werden.

Da die Aluminiumhaut mit ihrer Stringenz auf der gesamten Länge des Gebäudes sicherlich allzu provozierend gewesen wäre, wurde sie von den Architekten mit anderen Elementen geschickt „überspielt". Es entstand der abgesenkte Spielplatz der Erstklässler, der sich vor dem Gebäude zum Platz hin öffnet. Durch die Tieferlegung konnte außerdem ein weiteres Geschoß gewonnen werden. Auf diesen teilweise begrünten Platzraum haben die Passanten Einblick. So können die kleinen Kinder in den Pausen draußen in einem vom Stadtraum abgetrennten Freiraum spielen.

punched through the entire depth of the new building to create open-air play areas here, as there was not enough room on the ground. Finally, the entire length of the new building is topped by a flying roof, a rigged, white canvas structure that shades the roof terrace and its artificial lawn. This is the play area for the older children, also installed above the city for lack of space elsewhere.

The design concept for Nîmes demonstrates how Brunet and Saunier succeed in using a homogeneous, seemingly banal, repetitive structural system that appears to be taken from industrial building, in a new and persuasive way. Other examples, such as the school of music and dance in Le Havre, under construction at the time of writing, or the temporary building for Jussieu University completed in 1999, illustrate this quality with comparable facade concepts.

In Nîmes, the attitude, uncompromising and yet not in any way dominant, is decisive in making the building a surprise in this historic place. Because of its facade, some critics have put down the entire structure as being too crude, too technical. In

Eine weitere Maßnahme der Architekten, die Dominanz der Aluminiumlamellen zurückzunehmen, zeigt sich in der Fassade selbst. Zwei breite Öffnungen als eine Art Loggien, die die gesamte Tiefe der „Aufdoppelung" einnehmen, sind im ersten und zweiten Obergeschoß ausgelassen worden, um bei der begrenzt zur Verfügung stehenden Fläche Platz für Spielzonen an der frischen Luft zu schaffen. Als letzte Maßnahme schließlich erhielt der Bau das über allem hervorragende Flugdach, eine verspannte Konstruktion aus weißen Planen, die die Dachterrasse mit dem Kunststoffrasen-Pausenhof der größeren Kinder, der ebenfalls aus Platzgründen dort über der Stadt eingerichtet werden mußte, vor Sonnenstrahlen schützt.

Das Entwurfskonzept für Nîmes zeigt, wie es Brunet und Saunier gelingt, mit sicherer Hand ein homogenes, für sich betrachtet zunächst banal wirkendes, repetitiv eingesetztes Konstruktionssystem, das aus dem Industriebau zu stammen scheint, neu gesehen und überzeugend einzusetzen ist. Andere Beispiele wie die in Bau befindliche Musik- und Tanzschule in Le Havre und der 1999 in Paris realisierte provisorische Neubau für die Universität Jussieu verdeutlichen dies bei ihren Fassadenkonzepten in vergleichbarer Form.

the interplay of closure and transparency, however, it is conclusively structured and all its parts follow a clear functional logic. There is no conflict of scale, and in sunlight the building and its many delicate slats gleam like precious silver under the Mediterranean sky.

The exteriors of both the school, on a small scale, and of the Roman theatre, on a large scale, are transformed into sculptural framework. Naturally, the buildings are not comparable in terms of their physical presence in framing open space. A very different impression results in each. But in a purely formal sense, in both cases the effect is that of the interplay of interior and exterior. The arena's large arcades open the galleries to the exterior, the school's aluminium structure, extended far in front of the actual building, pulls together and structures the facade as a whole.

A second encounter will better illustrate how Brunet and Saunier master the work with reduced facade structures. We move from Nîmes, the city between the Cevennes and the Camargue, to Saint-Germain-en-Laye, a suburb north-west of Paris.

In Nîmes ist die kompromißlose Haltung, die dennoch keine Dominanz aufkommen läßt, das Bestimmende, das den Bau zu einer Überraschung an diesem historischen Ort macht. Mag die Kritik in bezug auf die Entscheidung für diese Fassade das gesamte Gebäude als zu derb, zu technisch abtun, es ist dennoch im Wechselspiel zwischen Geschlossenheit und Transparenz in sich schlüssig aufgebaut und folgt auch funktional unmißverständlich in allen Bereichen einer klaren Logik. Man gerät nicht in einen Konflikt hinsichtlich des Maßstabs. Und bei Sonne schimmert der Bau sogar mit seinem vielen feingliedrigen Lamellen kostbar silbrig unter dem mediterranen Himmel.

Obgleich die Begrenzungen der Räume keinesfalls dieselbe Präsenz haben, kann dennoch im kleinen bei der Schule wie auch im großen beim römischen Theater das Äußere in ein plastisches Gerüst überführt werden. Natürlich wird ein völlig anderes Bild geboten – und doch, rein formal ergibt sich bei beiden ein Zusammenspiel von Innen und Außen – hier die großen Arkaden der Arena, mit denen sich die Umgänge nach außen öffnen, und dort bei der Schule die weit vorgezogene Aluminiumstruktur, die die Fassade faßt und gliedert.

International School in
Saint-Germain-en-Laye

Die Internationale Schule
in Saint-Germain-en-Laye

Here Brunet and Saunier built another school. A direct comparison is interesting as the schools were realised at the same time, but based on entirely different concepts. The International School commanded a large estate with the Château d'Hennemont. The former working quarters located below the castle, as well as many other structures on the site, were already being used by the school. The working quarters consisted of two short two-storey wings with gable roofs and a lower connecting wing. The brief included some of the school's special functions: an auditorium, a restaurant and a library. In order to retain the character of the old ensemble, Brunet and Saunier chose not to touch the wings and to totally integrate the new rectangular building into the existing structure.

The architects refrained from doing too much. The special location, embedded in a park, surrounded by isolated historic buildings, and the direct extension to the remains of the existing structure in particular, called for a neutral solution with no need to flaunt itself. The architecture of the reinforced concrete skeleton with slender round columns is therefore emphasised only in the suspended glass skin. It is

Um ein klareres Bild zu erhalten, wie Brunet und Saunier mit reduzierten Fassadenstrukturen bei ihren Bauten und Projekten umzugehen wissen, sollte eine weitere Begegnung folgen. Bei dieser Begegnung geht es von Nîmes, der Stadt zwischen Cevennen und Camargue, in den nordwestlich von Paris gelegenen Vorort Saint-Germain-en-Laye. Hier haben Brunet und Saunier ebenfalls eine Schule errichtet. Der direkte Vergleich ist insoweit interessant, da hier zu gleicher Zeit ein Schulbau mit grundlegend anderer Konzeption entstand. Die Internationale Schule verfügte mit dem Château d'Hennemont bereits über ein großzügiges Anwesen am Ort. Unterhalb des Schlosses befindet sich ein Wirtschaftsgebäude, das wie auch weitere Bauten auf dem Terrain bereits für die Schule genutzt wurde. Dieses Wirtschaftsgebäude bestand aus zwei kurzen zweigeschossigen Flügelbauten mit Satteldach und einem mittleren, niedrigeren Quertrakt. Die Bauaufgabe umfaßte Sonderfunktionen der Schule: Aula, Restaurant und Bibliothek. Um den Charakter der alten Anlage zu bewahren, entschieden sich Brunet und Saunier, die Flügelbauten zu belassen und einen rechteckigen Neubaukomplex vollständig in den Bestand zu integrieren.

treated with particular attention and care. In contrast to the school in Nîmes, where the building structure is hidden by the slat wall, here the facade structure is immediately legible: it is a self-bearing fixed-panel window system with aluminium frames, completely prefabricated and made up of identical elements screwed to the concrete structure, similiar to Dominique Perrault's Hôtel Industriel "Jean-Baptiste Berlier" completed in 1990. Jérôme Brunet and Eric Saunier are friendly with Perrault. Years ago they took over his office space in Rue Vieille-du-Temple. What is new in the window system at Saint-Germain-en-Laye is the delicate sunscreen grating between the two layers of glass. It is a fixed perforated aluminium structure. It admits only subdued light because of its perforation, that texturally resembles cleaning tracks, but from close-up the view outside is hardly impaired. The ensuing character of a total enclosure is surprising. Only after some time does one grow accustomed to it, once seeing outside becomes possible from the right point of view. Seemingly different at first in terms of its organisation, the building does allow for a comparison to the school in Nîmes. In both cases, the architects chose a shading device that limits views into and out of the building. Here, however, this is

Die Architekten haben sich hier zurückgenommen. Der besondere Ort, eingebettet in eine Grünanlage, umgeben von vereinzelt stehenden historischen Bauten, und vor allem der direkte Anbau an die Reste der alten Querflügel ließ nach ihrer Meinung nur ein in seinem Äußeren neutrales Gebäude zu, das es nicht braucht, sich darzustellen. Seine Architektur, eine Stahlbeton-Skelettkonstruktion mit schlanken Rundstützen, zeigt sich daher ausschließlich in seiner vorgehängten Glashaut. Ihr gilt ein besonderes Augenmerk. Im Gegensatz zur Schule in Nîmes mit der vorgestellten Lamellen-Wand zeigt sich hier auf den ersten Blick der Aufbau eines selbsttragenden, festverglasten Fenstersystems mit Aluminiumrahmen, das in immer gleichen Elementen komplett vorgefertigt an die Betonkonstruktion geschraubt wurde, wie es zum Beispiel beim 1990 fertiggestellten Pariser Hôtel Industriel „Jean-Baptiste Berlier" von Dominique Perrault der Fall ist. Jérôme Brunet und Eric Saunier sind mit Perrault befreundet und waren einmal Nachmieter seiner Büroräume in der Rue Vieille-du-Temple. Neu sind bei dem festverglasten Fenstersystem in Saint-Germain-en-Laye die zwischen den beiden Scheiben liegenden, sehr feinen Sonnenschutzgitter. Es handelt sich dabei um eine perforierte Aluminiumkonstruktion, die nicht verstellbar ist. Einerseits läßt sie durch die Perforation, die in ihrer Struktur Putzschienen ähnelt, nur gedämpftes Licht hindurch, andererseits ist beim näheren Herantre-

achieved not by two separate facades placed side by side, but by one compact space-saving system that integrates the different layers. In contrast to Nîmes, blocking direct sunlight only in the window element itself was a disadvantage. It resulted in excessive heating of the building's southern side and required the installation of a second shading device later.

The sober box in the upscale suburb of Saint-Germain-en-Laye, mirroring in daylight, transparent at night, is controversial among the teachers. In good weather, many feel locked up inside the building, which is understandable, located, as they are, in the middle of a park. But regardless of one's judgement of the smooth skin: with the facade, Brunet and Saunier are once again breaking new ground. Doing so inevitably entails fundamental discussions.

The narrow slats at Nîmes, the delicate aluminium grating integrated into the glass in Saint-Germain-en-Laye, but also the angled industrial glass elements set in front of the facade at Jussieu University in Paris, make one thing clear: the architects are

ten der Blick nach draußen so gering wie möglich beeinträchtigt. Diese durchgehende Abschottung verwundert. Erst nach einer gewissen Zeit tritt die Gewöhnung ein, dann nämlich, wenn bei richtigem Blickwinkel der Ausblick gut möglich ist. Was sich zunächst von seinem Aufbau her ganz anders ansah, läßt nun doch eine gewisse Parallele zur Schule in Nîmes erkennen. Denn wieder wurde von den Architekten ein Sonnenschutzsystem gewählt, das den freien Aus- und Einblick nur in einem begrenzten Rahmen zuläßt. Hier sind es allerdings keine zwei völlig getrennt nebeneinander stehenden Fassaden, sondern es ist ein kompaktes, sehr platzsparendes System, das die einzelnen Schichten integriert. Nachteilig wirkt, daß die Sonneneinstrahlung im Unterschied zu Nîmes erst im Fensterelement selbst verhindert wird. Dadurch entstand auf der Südseite des Gebäudes eine zu große Aufheizung. So mußte hier nachträglich eine weitere Sonnenschutzvorrichtung installiert werden.

Der nüchterne, tagsüber spiegelnde, bei Dunkelheit transparente Kasten im noblen Vorort Saint-Germain-en-Laye ist bei den Lehrern umstritten. Viele fühlen sich bei schönem Wetter in dem Gebäude zu sehr eingeschlossen. Inmitten eines Parks ist dies allzu gut ver-

working on new variations of the visual effects that result from the specific use of materials. Proximity and distance, angle of vision and light create varying textures. The observer sees something different time and again, sometimes even believes in optical illusions.

Two visits marked the beginning of this reflection. They were chance encounters in different places. The school buildings caught the eye and stimulate interest in studying the work of the two architects more closely.

ständlich. Dennoch, wie immer man diese glatte Fassadenhaut auch bewerten mag: Auch hier haben Brunet und Saunier bei der Fassade den Schritt in ein Neuland gewagt, der zwangsläufig zu grundsätzlichen Diskussionen führt.

Die schmalen Lamellen in Nîmes, das feine, in das Glas integrierte Aluminiumraster in Saint-Germain-en-Laye, aber auch die schräg vorgestellten Industrieglas-Elemente bei der Fassade der Bauten für die Universität Jussieu in Paris lassen eines deutlich erkennen: Die Architekten erarbeiten neue Variationen der visuellen Wirkung, die sich durch die gezielte Einsetzung der Materialien ergeben. Nähe und Weite, der Blickwinkel und das Licht offerieren unterschiedliche Strukturen. Der Betrachter sieht immer wieder etwas anderes, glaubt manchmal sogar an eine optische Täuschung.

Zwei Besuche standen zu Beginn der Betrachtung. Es waren zufällige Begegnungen an verschiedenen Orten. Die Schulbauten haben den Blick geschärft und reizen, sich nun mit der Arbeit der beiden Architekten näher zu befassen.

School of Music, Chalon-sur-Saône, facade detail.

Fassadendetail der Musikschule in Chalon-sur-Saône

Residential building Rue
Neuve Tolbiac in Paris

Wohnblock Rue Neuve
Tolbiac in Paris

the available means proves that here an idea was pursued and followed through up to the realisation of the details, while in other projects it had not been possible to allot similar attention to detailing. In Montpellier, Ludwig Mies van der Rohe's Barcelona Pavilion was the model: not in scale, not in terms of function, but in the basic conception of the wall and floor slabs with the flowing, celebratory and stately space. The degree to which Mies van der Rohe's work serves as an example to the architects is apparent in other projects also – particularily in the secondary school in Rozay-en-Brie. In the Montpellier bank, the elegant, clearly legible and apparently isolated wall slabs create the basic structure of the banking hall. The adjacent building, not accessible to the public, has an entirely different, independent quality. Its glass skin has since been employed as a well-tried facade composition – in variations and with other detail solutions – in subsequent projects like the residential building on Rue Neuve Tolbiac in Paris, or the office building project for Angers, a competition prize of 1999.

Architekten zu stammen scheint. Brunet und Saunier verteidigen ihren hier gewählten „Stil", indem sie den Standpunkt vertreten, sich der Konsequenz der Aufgabe gestellt zu haben. In der Anwendung der zur Verfügung stehenden Mittel wird auch sichtbar, daß hier eine Idee weiterverfolgt und bis in die Details, die bei manchen anderen Projekten nicht die gewünschte Qualität erfahren konnten, umgesetzt wurde. In Montpellier stand Mies van der Rohe mit seinem Barcelona-Pavillon Pate: nicht im Maßstab, auch nicht unter funktionaler Sicht, sondern in der Grundkonzeption der Wand- und Deckenscheiben mit dem fließenden, festlich-repräsentativen Raum. Wie stark die Arbeit Mies van der Rohes bei den Architekten als Vorbild gesehen wird, zeigt sich auch in anderen Zusammenhängen – vor allem bei der realisierten Oberschule in Rozay-en-Brie. Bei der Bank in Montpellier bilden die eleganten, klar ablesbaren und scheinbar isoliert stehenden Wandscheiben die Grundstruktur der Kassenhalle. Der seitlich stehende Gebäuderiegel, der nicht für den Publikumsverkehr zugänglich ist, hat hingegen eine eigene, ganz andere Qualität. Es ist die gläserne Haut, die in Variationen und mit anderen Antworten im Detail auch bei anderen Bauten wie dem Wohnblock in der Rue Neuve Tolbiac in Paris oder beim Bürohaus-Projekt für Angers – ein Wettbewerbserfolg von 1999 – als inzwischen bewährte Fassadenkomposition eingesetzt wird.

Angers gilt es als einen besonderen Entwurf der Architekten hervorzuheben. Hier manifestiert sich ein neuartiges Konzept für den Bürobau, das an den zahlreichen Studien der letzten Jahrzehnte zum Thema „offenes Büro" oder „Kombibüro" anknüpft. Die Fassade ist als

Following page:
The secondary school
of Rozay-en-Brie

Folgende Seite:
Die Oberschule in
Rozay-en-Brie

Angers should be noted as an exceptional design in the architects' œuvre. A new concept for office construction emerges here, pursuing the endeavours of recent decades on topics like the "open office". The facade is to be read as an immaterial "protective envelope". While the actual offices are inserted into a frame-like structure. The system can be seen as a type of "house-in-house" where individual duplex units make up the building volume. The parts are flexible, some projecting slightly from the facade, and can be recombined at any time.

The building where site is best discussed, but also in the most contradictory terms, is located on Rue de Flandre in the 19th arrondissement of Paris. In the sixties, the road, dead straight, was widened on its north side, in the course of which numerous turn-of-the-century buildings were demolished and replaced by high housing blocks which only partially follow the new street line. On the south side of the road, where the new building is located, a few big blocks were added, set back from the street between existing buildings. As a result of the ensuing disparities in scale, the street has assumed unusual urban form. With their corner building, Brunet and Saunier

entmaterialisierter „Schutzumschlag" zu verstehen. Die Büroräume sind in eine gerüstartige Konstruktion eingefügt. Man kann das System als eine Art „Haus-in-Haus"-Konzept in einzelnen Maisonetten begreifen, aus denen sich der Riegel zusammensetzt. Die Teile sind flexibel, schieben sich zum Teil auch leicht aus der Fassade hervor und sind jederzeit anders zu kombinieren.

Das Gebäude, bei dem der Ort am deutlichsten, aber auch am widersprüchlichsten diskutiert werden kann, steht an der Rue de Flandre im 19. Pariser Arrondissement. In den sechziger Jahren erfuhr die schnurgerade Straße an ihrer Nordseite eine Verbreiterung, für die ganze Häuserzeilen der Jahrhundertwende abgebrochen und durch hohe Wohnblocks ersetzt wurden, die nur teilweise der neuen Straßenflucht folgen. Auf der Südseite mit dem Neubau wurden, von der Flucht zurückgesetzt, nur ein paar große Blocks zwischen Altbauten eingefügt. Die Straße hat mit diesen Maßstabssprüngen eine ungewöhnliche stadträumliche Gestalt angenommen. So versuchen Brunet und Saunier mit ihrem Eckgebäude diese Struktur etwas auszugleichen. Sie unternahmen an diesem Ort den Versuch, die Typologie des Pariser Faubourg-Gebäudes neu zu übersetzen. Schon Aldo Rossi machte sich Ende der achtziger Jahren zum Thema, den Typus des klassischen Pariser Hauses neu zu interpretieren, als er beauftragt wurde, ganz in der Nähe von der Rue de Flandre in La Villette einen

Facade detail of residential block Rue de Flandre in Paris

Fassadendetail des Wohnblocks Rue de Flandre in Paris

Facade detail of residential
building Rue Neuve Tolbiac
in Paris

Fassadendetail des Wohn-
blocks Rue Neuve Tolbiac
in Paris

tried to balance this structure. They attempted a new translation of the typology of the Parisian Faubourg building. In the late eighties, Aldo Rossi had already made it his theme to reinterpret the classical Parisian house. At the time, he was commissioned to design a residential building near Rue de Flandre in La Villette, next to Christian de Portzamparc's music school. Rossi's building is characterized by high mansard roofs and an open gallery with tightly positioned columns on the ground floor. According to the architect, it should recall Rue de Rivoli, and in so doing, the building is to a have "a greater effect on the city than buildings of the avantgarde". The concept was a failure, as we know today. The building shows no typological progression, and perseveres in a theoretical, very questionable image. In plan, the flats have no demonstrable qualities, and the arcades are of no real use.

This is different in Brunet and Saunier's residential building. The street facade on Rue de Flandre is characterised by impressive elegance. Here the reaction to the site is not an isolated gesture, but refers directly to the neighbourhood. The building is not a symbol, placed there to send us a message, but becomes an integral part

Wohnblock neben die Musikschule von Christian de Portzamparc zu stellen. Bei Rossis Bau werden hohe Mansarddächer erkennbar und eine offene Passage mit eng gestellter Stützenreihe im Erdgeschoß, die – so der Architekt – an die Rue de Rivoli erinnern soll. Damit soll der Bau „eine größere Wirkung auf die Stadt haben als Bauwerke der Avantgarde". Ein gescheitertes Konzept, wie wir heute wissen. Das Gebäude stellt typologisch keine Weiterentwicklung dar und verharrt damit in einem theoretischen, sehr fragwürdigen Bild. Die Grundrisse der Wohnungen haben keine vorzeigbaren Qualitäten, und der Arkadengang hat kein brauchbares Nutzungskonzept.

Dies ist anders bei dem Wohngebäude von Brunet und Saunier. Die Straßenfassade in der Rue de Flandre weist eine eindruckvolle Eleganz auf. Hier ist die Reaktion auf den Ort nicht isoliert zu sehen, sondern nimmt direkten Bezug auf die Nachbarschaft. Das Haus ist kein Symbol, das für sich steht und etwas mitteilt, sondern fügt sich wie selbstverständlich in das Gefüge ein. Die Großzügigkeit und Klarheit, die die Fassade ausstrahlt, setzt sich allerdings nicht in der Organisation der Wohnungen fort. Die Bezüge zu Haussmann wirken von innen gesehen auf den Betrachter gezwungen. Dennoch ist auch dies eine Arbeit, die mutig neue Wege versucht hat – und hinten, auf engsten Raum an diesem schwierigen Ort, neben einem alten Viadukt und mit problematischer Belichtung, haben die Architekten das Beste erreichen können, was möglich war.

of the texture. Admittedly, the largesse and clarity of the facade is not carried through to the organisation of the flats. Seen from the inside, the references to Haussmann seem forced. Nevertheless, the project dared to go new paths – and in the back, in the tightest part on this difficult site, next to the old viaduct, with problematic lighting conditions, the architects achieved best possible work.

This approach is not based on pure joy of experimentation, which would have to be viewed critically. There is no room for experimentation in this kind of design problem. Brunet and Saunier, however, do have the tenacity to engage in a given problem. And yet, in comparison, their great success in housing is the new residential building on Rue Neuve Tolbiac. The site allowed for little liberty, as the urban development was already laid down in a masterplan by Roland Schweitzer. It was to be a "building exhibition": different residential blocks, among others by Francis Soler and Philippe Gazeau, are to surround Dominique Perrault's Bibliothèque Nationale de France. Once again, the building is captivating in the largesse of the facades. The glass building is reminiscent of the sixties and seventies, a period that the architects like to refer to, more so than to the twenties and thirties.

Es handelt sich nicht um eine Experimentierfreude, die kritisch zu beurteilen wäre. Experimentieren sollte man bei einer solchen Aufgabe nicht. Brunet und Saunier haben aber die Ausdauer, sich der Aufgabe anzunehmen. Im Vergleich gesehen ist dann aber doch der Neubau an der Rue Neuve Tolbiac als der große Wurf im Bereich des Wohnungsbaus anzusehen. Der Ort ließ wenig Spielraum, die stadträumliche Anordnung war bereits durch einen Bebauungsplan von Roland Schweitzer festgelegt worden. Thema war eine „Bauausstellung": Verschiedene Wohnblocks, unter anderem auch von Francis Soler und Philippe Gazeau, sollen Dominique Perraults Bibliothèque Nationale de France umgeben. Auch hier besticht der Bau durch die bei den Fassaden erkennbare Großzügigkeit. Es handelt sich um einen Glasbau, der an die sechziger und siebziger Jahre erinnert, eine Zeit, an die die Architekten gerne anknüpfen – eher als an die zwanziger und dreißiger Jahre.

Serigraphic fragments of texts by Jean Anouilh and Pierre Choderlos de Laclos were applied on the balcony parapets of the residential building Rue Neuve Tolbiac

Auf den Brüstungen des Wohnblocks Rue Neuve Tolbiac sind serigraphisch Bruchstücke aus Texten von Jean Anouilh und Pierre Choderlos de Laclos aufgebracht worden

In what different ways Brunet and Saunier deal with site is also demonstrated by two hospital projects. The projects for Caen and Tours are examples of a changed philosophy of clinic construction in France. New clinics are once again being located close to the inner city in order to better integrate them. The pediatric hospital in Caen, in particular, is no longer to be a refuge for "outcasts", but a largely open place of public passage. The building extends north-south between the wide Avenue Georges-Clémenceau and the remains of an old park and an existing birth clinic. The new building is organised in cross shape, permitting access from all sides. In Caen, the average number of annual rain days is 184. Large roofs covering the exterior areas are a special feature. There will be a patio where patients can play with visiting friends, turning the hospital into a children's house. An open-air theatre has also been planned. Outdoor roofing comprises 28 square umbrellas with textile membranes. The facades of the two long building fronts each consist of one enormous steel frame. Each frame borders a grid of flat panels made either of light stone from the Caen region or of glass. Windows shift from children's to adults' eye-height in order to create a vivid picture.

Wie unterschiedlich Brunet und Saunier auf den Ort reagieren, zeigt sich auch bei zwei Projekten im Bereich Krankenhausbau. Die Projekte für Caen und Tours stehen beispielhaft für eine veränderte Konzeption beim Neubau von Kliniken in Frankreich. Man hat sich darauf besonnen, die Bauten wieder soweit möglich nahe der Innenstadt zu bauen und somit besser zu integrieren. Besonders das Kinderkrankenhaus in Caen soll kein Refugium für „Ausgeschlossene" mehr sein, sondern ein weitgehend offener Ort der Passage für alle. Das Gebäude erstreckt sich von Norden nach Süden zwischen der breiten Avenue Georges-Clémenceau und Resten einer alten Parkanlage sowie einer vorhandenen Geburtsklinik. Der Neubau ist in Form eines Kreuzes organisiert, das die Erschließung von allen Seiten her ermöglicht. In Caen regnet es im Durchschnitt 184 Tage im Jahr. Eine Besonderheit des Projekts ist die weite Überdachung der Außenbereiche. Es wird ein Patio entstehen, wo kranke Kinder mit ihren zu Besuch kommenden Freunden spielen können. Das Krankenhaus wird zum Kinderhaus. Auch an ein Freilufttheater ist gedacht. Die Überdachung besteht aus 28 quadratischen Schirmen mit textiler Bespannung. Die Fassaden der beiden Längsseiten des Krankenhauses bestehen aus je einem riesigen Stahlrahmen, in dem flache gerasterte Felder entweder mit hellen Steinplatten aus der Gegend von Caen oder mit Glasflächen versehen werden. Durch den Wechsel der Fensteranordnung in Augenhöhe der Kinder oder der Erwachsenen soll sich ein abwechselungsreiches Bild ergeben.

Project for the university
hospital of Caen

Projekt für das Universi-
tätskrankenhaus von Caen

Project for the tax office
in Nîmes

Projekt für das Finanzamt
in Nîmes

44

Jérôme Brunet and Eric Saunier do not consider themselves to belong to a "brotherhood" of architecture. They do not want to be "servants of faith" of a particular "order", characterised by its unmistakable outer appearance. And again, the conversation with them focuses on their favourite topic: the uncompromising rejection of a dogmatic, definitive line in their architecture. They want to be able to deal freely with the few recurring elements and solve every problem with a new approach, while not treading paths that are too unconventional. The declared goal is to retain a measure of freedom in order to offer sufficient flexibility. This may sound easy, but it is also challenging. It probably guarantees that in the conceptual phase, the playful aspect of their work is not neglected.

Balance | Die Balance

Jérôme Brunet und Eric Saunier sehen sich mit ihrer Architektur nicht als „Mönche". Sie wollen keine „Glaubensdiener" eines bestimmten „Ordens" sein, der sich unmißverständlich durch seine äußerliche Gestalt zu erkennen gibt. Wieder fokussiert sich das Gespräch mit ihnen auf ihr bevorzugtes Thema: die kompromißlose Ablehnung einer dogmatischen, eindeutig zu definierenden Linie in ihrer Architektur. Mit den wenigen wiederkehrenden Elementen wollen sie frei umgehen können und jede neue Aufgabe mit einem eigenen Ansatz lösen, ohne allerdings allzu eigenwillige Wege zu beschreiten. Das klar bekundete Ziel ist, eine Freiheit zu bewahren, um damit genügend Flexibilität zu bieten. Dies klingt einfach, fordert aber auch heraus und läßt es wohl zu, daß in der Konzeptphase das spielerische Element nicht zu kurz kommt.

Considering the œuvre as a whole and studying the ideas sketches produced in the design process, it is striking that next to the reference to site, the facade design is unusually important. Conceptual considerations in plan or spatial relationships are always thought of in terms of their relation to the facade. This is not to say that the "clothing" supersedes what is essential – such an assumption would miss the point of the architects' work. But the spatial organisation does not usually seem as imaginatively or ingeniousely worked out as the conception for the facade. This is especially evident in examples such as the school in Saint-Germain-en-Laye or the rehabilitation clinic for children in Palavas-les-Flots.

In housing construction, which to date has all been subsidised projects in Paris, there is even a certain discrepancy between the facade and the flats. The building volume on Rue Neuve Tolbiac with its 95 units is extremely elegant and draws visitors into surprisingly spatious entrance lobbies, open across the entire building depth. The upper stories, however, are characterised by narrow, dark interior hallways. Clearly, the building was conceived for the glass skin. Because of this, some

Betrachtet man die Bauten und Projekte im Ganzen und studiert die Ideenskizzen der Entstehungsgeschichte eines Entwurfs, so fällt auf, daß nach der Bezugnahme zum Ort die Fassadengestaltung einen ungewöhnlich großen Stellenwert einnimmt. Konzeptuelle Überlegungen bei den Grundrissen und Raumzusammenhängen sind sehr stark in einem Bezug zur Fassade zu lesen. Damit soll nicht behauptet werden, daß das „Kleid" das Wesentliche zurückdrängt. Damit würde man den Architekten nicht gerecht werden. Aber die Planung der räumlichen Zuordnungen scheint meist lange nicht so ideenreich und raffiniert durchdacht zu sein wie das Fassadenkonzept. Dies wird zum Beispiel bei dem Schulbau in Saint-Germain-en-Laye oder der Reha-Klinik für Kinder in Palavas-les-Flots deutlich.

Im Wohnungsbau, bei dem es sich bisher ausschließlich um staatliche geförderte Projekte in Paris handelte, wird sogar eine gewisse Diskrepanz zwischen Fassade und Wohnung deutlich. Mag der Gebäuderiegel mit 95 Wohnungen an der Rue Neuve Tolbiac noch eine solche Eleganz ausstrahlen und den Besucher zunächst in eine auffallend großzügige, die gesamte Tiefe des Riegels einnehmende Eingangshalle führen, so folgt in den Obergeschossen ein beengter, dunkler Erschließungs-Innenflur. Ohne Zweifel ist das Haus in seiner

flats are at a disadvantage. Those that span the depth of the building, for example, are somewhat cornered in parts – the living areas, extending directly on to the surrounding balconies thanks to the large sliding doors, dominate everything else. Because of the restricting brief it was not possible to achieve here an innovative conception for housing construction was not achieved. Rather, the priority was the attractive idea of having a glass facade across from the Bibliothèque Nationale de France, with serigraphically applied fragments of texts by Jean Anouilh and Pierre Choderlos de Laclos.

In Rue de Flandre, the discrepancy between the facade and the spatial quality of the flats is even more obvious. Brunet and Saunier opted for a facade that could almost be labeled "classical", unusual for their practice. But the large French windows with their white sliding shutters are not only a part of the facade: added in long rows, they are themselves the facade, creating a diversified picture. They are separated only by the narrow horizontal bands of the floor slabs. From the outside, once again, the image of social housing has been dispelled. The building fits into the old street-

ganzen Konzeption auf die gläserne Haut hin konzipiert. Manche Wohnungen haben dadurch sogar Nachteile. Die blockdurchgreifenden Wohnungen zum Beispiel sind in Teilbereichen etwas verwinkelt – alles wird beherrscht von den Aufenthaltsbereichen, die aufgrund der großen Schiebetüren direkt in die umlaufenden Balkone übergehen. Hier ist nicht ein innovatives Grundkonzept im Wohnungsbau entwickelt worden, dafür waren die Vorgaben zu sehr festgelegt. Vielmehr stand die gläserne Fassade mit der schönen Idee, gegenüber der Bibliothèque Nationale de France die gläsernen Balkonbrüstungen mit Textfragmenten von Jean Anouilh und Pierre Choderlos de Laclos serigraphisch zu gestalten, im Vordergrund.

Bei dem Beispiel Rue de Flandre ist diese Diskrepanz zwischen Fassade und Raumqualität bei den Wohnungen noch augenscheinlicher. Brunet und Saunier haben hier in einer für ihr Büro ungewöhnlichen Entwurfssprache eine fast schon „klassisch" zu bezeichnende Fassadenstruktur gewählt. Die großen französischen Fenster mit ihren weißen Schiebe-Läden sind aber nicht nur ein Bestandteil der Fassade, sie selbst bilden, in langen Reihen nebeneinander gefügt, die Fassade und sorgen für ein abwechslungsreiches Bild. In der

Following page:
Facade detail of the rehabilitation clinic for children in Palavas-les-Flots

Folgende Seite:
Fassadenausschnitt der Reha-Klinik für Kinder in Palavas-les-Flots

Pergola at the entrance to
the rehabilitation clinic

Pergola am Eingang der
Reha-Klinik

front of a side street, but compared to earlier social housing programs in the area, it resembles luxury condominiums and is clearly set apart. This concerns only the building's exterior. The interior is a more complicated matter. For what appears on the outside turns out to be very different on the inside. The architects designed a window that crosses floor levels. The continuous floor levels so strongly articulated on the outside therefore do not actually correspond to the height of the structural floor slabs behind. The difference of a bit less than half a metre means that the upper zone of every French window, covering the actual floor behind, is made of dark mirrored glass, but hardly read as such from the outside. The band in the facade must therefore be interpreted as the parapet. Because a parapet must be one metre high, an additional pane of glass had to be added in front of the windows. Nevertheless, the actual window is still two metres high, and the floor to ceiling height is 2.60 metres.

Horizontalen werden sie nur durch schmale Geschoßdeckenbänder unterbrochen. Auch hier ist in der äußeren Erscheinung das Image vom sozialen Wohnungsbau wie weggewischt. Das Gebäude paßt sich in die alte Gebäudefront einer Querstraße ein, fällt aber im Vergleich zu früheren Wohnblocks in der Umgebung mit staatlich geförderten Wohnungen deutlich als eine fast schon luxuriöse Wohnanlage heraus. Dies ist nur das Äußere des Gebäudes. Innen ist die Sache komplizierter. Denn was beim ersten Eindruck vermutet wird, zeigt sich innen ganz anders: Die Architekten haben sich für eine geschoßübergreifende Fenster-Konzeption entschieden. Die außen durchlaufenden, besonders hervorgehobenen Geschoßebenen entsprechen nicht der Höhe der inneren Decken. Der Versatz von einem knappen halben Meter führt dazu, daß die obere Glaszone jedes französischen Fensters, hinter der sich die eigentliche Decke befindet, aus dunklem Spiegelglas besteht, das außen als solches kaum auszumachen ist. Das äußere Band in der Fassade ist daher als Brüstungsabschluß zu begreifen. Da die Brüstung eine Höhe von einem Meter aufweisen muß, wurde oberhalb dieses Streifens noch eine Glasscheibe vor die Fenster gesetzt. Das Fenster selbst hat noch eine Höhe von zwei Metern. Innen ergibt sich eine lichte Geschoßhöhe von 2,60 Metern.

In Rue de Flandre, for the first time something occurs that is foreign to the work of Brunet and Saunier. The facade claims to be something that does not match the interior. The qualities of the building, well-proportioned and well-adapted to the ensemble in Rue de Flandre, are unquestioned. Also, the idea of working with the Faubourg-era building type may certainly create exciting possibilities in facade design. But their concept leaves one puzzled. Here they have, for the first time, designed a "skin" that in a sense does not want to go beyond being a show facade. This is a departure from the position they usually defend with such clarity. Brunet and Saunier's position that they do not want to be categorised and that they begin every design problem on a new premise leaves one at a loss here, as for the first time the architects have moved in a direction that does not match their hand. As in Rue Neuve Tolbiac, little space remained for circulation on the upper floors. The flats themselves are tight, their spatial organisation is simple and they conform to social housing guidelines. The best possible solutions were achieved by rearranging the available surface areas. The two top floors were even made into duplex flats.

In der Rue de Flandre geschieht zum ersten Mal etwas für Brunet und Sauniers Arbeit Fremdes. Die Fassade täuscht etwas vor, was mit dem Inneren nicht zusammenpaßt. Die Qualitäten des gut proportionierten und auch gut in das Ensemble an der Rue de Flandre eingepaßten Gebäudes steht außer Frage. Auch die Idee, sich mit dem Haustyp der Faubourg zu befassen, mag sicherlich bei der Fassade spannungsvolle Möglichkeiten der Gestaltung bieten, aber das gewählte Konzept verwundert doch. Sie haben hier zum ersten Mal eine „Haut" gestaltet, die eigentlich nur als Schaufassade etwas darstellen will – und dies entspricht nicht ihrer Linie, die sie sonst mit solcher Klarheit vertreten. Brunet und Sauniers Hinweis, daß sie sich nicht einordnen lassen wollen und jede Aufgabe mit neuen Ansätzen beginnen, läßt einen hier ratlos. Denn die Architekten beschritten zum ersten Mal einen Weg, der nicht zu ihrer Handschrift paßt.

Für die Erschließungszonen in den Obergeschossen blieb wie in der Rue Neuve Tolbiac nur wenig Platz. Die Wohnungen selbst sind knapp und in ihren Raumzuordnungen einfach konzipiert. Sie tragen den Richtlinien des sozialen Wohnungsbaus Rechnung. Das Best-

Within Brunet and Saunier's range of architectural expression – never influenced by fashionable trends, not even in the case of Rue de Flandre – there is a general tendency to use the facade as an important element of transformation. A clearly dominant facade structure, more precisely a facade texture, is of great significance to the overall design. In some projects, the music centre in Le Havre for instance, the facade is so dominant that the actual structure or organisation of the building can no longer be made out. The reasons are well-known: the building is to represent itself. The architects prefer to lend their buildings an abstract quality, to supply them with a neutral layer they like to refer to as *enveloppe*. This layer as "cover" is not only distinct from the actual structure, in many examples it is in fact set in front of the building. Some people may feel inclined to get out their wire clippers to "liberate" the school children from behind the aluminium facade in Nîmes, or may want to remove some of the wooden slats from the base of the rehabilitation clinic in Palavas-les-Flots, but this would be wrong. Behind the idea of the *enveloppes* there is a design technique: the abstract skin creates a subtly proportioned building, gives it a face and makes it unique. The cover is both filter and protection.

mögliche wurde erreicht, indem man die zur Verfügung stehenden Flächen etwas anders aufteilte. In den beiden obersten Geschossen ergaben sich sogar Maisonettewohnungen.

In der Bandbreite des architektonischen Ausdrucks von Brunet und Saunier, der sich – und dies ist auch in der Rue de Flandre der Fall – von modischen Tendenzen unbeeinfußt zeigt, ist eine generelle Tendenz zu erkennen, die Fassade als ein wichtiges Element der Transformation einzusetzen. Gemeint ist damit, daß bewußt eine sich deutlich hervorhebende Fassadenstruktur, mehr noch eine Fassadentextur, in der Gesamtgestaltung einen hohen Stellenwert einnimmt. Sie prägt bei manchen Projekten, wie zum Beispiel dem Musikzentrum in Le Havre, das gesamte Gebäude in einem Maß, daß kein konkreter Aufbau mehr abzulesen ist. Die Gründe sind bekannt: Das Gebäude soll sich darstellen. Die Architekten neigen dazu, ihre Gebäude zu abstrahieren, sie mit einer neutralen Schicht zu versehen, die sie gerne als „Enveloppe" bezeichnen. Diese Schicht als „Hülle" setzt sich nicht nur vom eigentlichen konstruktiven Aufbau ab, sie steht bei zahlrei-

Without prejudice to its qualities, the "double shell" also has its problems. It creates a certain dissolution or a reduction of the observers' accustomed image of a building. In Palavas-les-Flots, this is apparent in the powerful basestorey on the beach. The horizontal wooden slats, formally joined in an extraordinarily elegant manner, ensure that from the outside one hardly catches a glimpse of what is going on inside the medicinal baths and the gymnastics rooms behind. In Jussieu, the university campus in southwestern Paris, the double shell was realized on a far more basic level. In these temporary buildings, the vertical industrial glass elements were simply set in front of the facade and screwed in. The architects again succeeded in creating an exciting visual stimulus, but the downside of the design is revealed, just as in Palavas-les-Flots, when seen up close: the building itself is not really present. The outer facades are visible, while the inner facade and interspace of the building behind can barely be made out. What happens to this space in between? What are the specific qualities of such a zone? How is the space, often up to sixty centimetres wide, cleaned, for example? These questions come to mind, but are quickly forgot-

chen Beispielen auch tatsächlich vor dem eigentlichen Gebäude. Man mag bei der Aluminumfassade der Schule in Nîmes geneigt sein, mit der Drahtschere vorzugehen, um die Kinder „zu befreien", oder bei der Reha-Klinik in Palavas-les-Flots manche Holzbretter des Sockelgeschosses zu lösen, aber dies wäre falsch. Denn hinter diesem Konzept der „Enveloppes" verbirgt sich eine Entwurfstechnik: Die abstrakte Haut macht aus dem Gebäude einen geschickt proportionierten Bau, gibt ihm ein Gesicht und etwas Unverwechselbares. Die Hülle ist zudem Filter und Schutz.

Unabhängig davon ist aber diese „Doppelschaligkeit" auch mit Problemen behaftet. Sie sorgt für eine gewisse Auflösung oder auch Reduzierung eines für den Betrachter vertrauten Bildes von einem Gebäude. In Palavas-les-Flots wird dies beim mächtigen Sockelgeschoß am Strand erkennbar. Die waagerecht, formal von außerordentlicher Eleganz gefügten Holzbretter sorgen dafür, daß kaum ein Einblick in die medizinischen Bäder und Turnräume der Klinik gewährt wird. In Jussieu, dem Universitätsgelände im Pariser Südosten, ist die Doppelschaligkeit auf einer viel einfacheren Ebene entstanden. Bei diesem provisorischen Bau sind die senkrechten Industrieglaselemente einfach davorgestellt und verschraubt worden. Auch hier gelingt ein spannungsvoller optischer Reiz, aber der Preis einer solchen Konzeption zeigt sich wie in Palavas-les-Flots, wenn man die Bauten aus der Nähe betrachtet. Das Gebäude selbst ist nicht wirklich

Facade of the university building on the Jussieu campus in Paris

Fassade des Universitätsgebäudes auf dem Campus von Jussieu in Paris

ten, when, at a distance, one becomes aware of the building's overall structure as a successful composition. The sight of Jussieu, very different depending on point of view and light of day, can be almost mystical.

One may wonder where this textural conception of facades will take us. The impression may occur that the momentum of permanence, so important in architecture, is missing here, generating doubts as to some of the buildings and projects. Nothing seems organic or massive. These qualities, intrinsic to building and lending it stability, are missing. Visual stability is not the subject of Brunet and Saunier. But even this certain discomfort is dispelled at the latest once the homogeneous structure of a facade is exposed in all its elegance and rich complexity. Not one of the facades needs a powerful gesture or a complicated, high-tech, stainless steel construction with its fake fragility to lend the building a strung-up dynamic touch. Brunet and Saunier do without superficially emblematic or structuralist elements.

präsent. Zu sehen sind die vorgestellten Fassaden, das eigentliche Gebäude dahinter mit einer weiteren Fassade und dessen Zwischenraum, zeigt sich kaum. Was passiert mit diesem Zwischenraum? Welche Qualität hat eine solche Zone? Wie werden die ungenutzten immerhin bis zu sechzig Zentimeter zum Beispiel gereinigt? Diese Fragen stellen sich, geraten aber bald darauf wieder in Vergessenheit, wenn man sich wieder vom Gebäude entfernt und die Gesamtstruktur als gelungene Komposition wahrnimmt. In Jussieu hat die Ansicht, die je nach Standpunkt und Sonnenlicht so stark changiert, fast schon etwas Mystisches.

Man mag darüber nachdenken, wohin diese Textur-Konzeption bei den Fassaden führen mag. Vielleicht entsteht der Eindruck, daß hier das für die Architektur so wichtige Moment der Dauerhaftigkeit fehlt, so daß Zweifel an manchen Bauten und Projekten aufkommt. Es ist nichts Gewachsenes und Schweres zu erkennen, das zum Bauen dazugehört und Halt gibt. Mit dem Auge erfahrbare Standfestigkeit ist nicht das Thema von Brunet und Saunier. Aber auch dieses gewisse Unbehagen ist spätestens dann wieder schnell verflogen, wenn sich vor einem die homogene Gesamtstruktur einer Fassade in ihrer ganzen Eleganz und Vielschichtigkeit zeigt. Sie hat es bei keinem der

Facade detail of the International School in Saint-Germain-en-Laye

Fassadendetail der Internationalen Schule in Saint-Germain-en-Laye

No part of the facades is tensioned, no detail is artfully crafted for purely aesthetic reasons. None of the formal elements are inventions. They all result from the work with existing materials. Wooden planks, aluminium slats and above all glass – glass columns in the Saint-Germain-en-Laye town hall, the glass roof of the Louvre workshops – are used in a way that the desired effect is created only by the particular treatment and joining of the materials.

This undogmatic and direct manner, never monotonous or exchangeable, characterises the work of Jérôme Brunet and Eric Saunier. This is what makes them so engaging. Heterogeneity, individuality and a certain measure of conceptual contradiction seem to be an integral part of their work. And one feels moved to forgive the sound of the wooden sliding doors, which form the most exposed facade layer in Palavas-les-Flots, forever grinding slightly in the floor tracks filled with sand blown over from the beach.

Bauten nötig, mit kraftvoller Geste aufzutrumpfen oder eine komplizierte, oft nur künstlich fragil wirkende High-Tech-Konstruktion aus Edelstahl aufzuweisen, die einem Gebäude eine überdrehte Dynamik geben. Brunet und Saunier kommen ohne das vordergründig Emblematische oder Strukturalistische aus. Nichts wird bei den Fassaden verspannt, kein Detail kunstvoll ausformuliert um der Gestaltung willen. Nichts wird an formalen Dingen neu erfunden, sondern mit dem Gegebenen an Materialien gearbeitet. Holzbretter, Aluminiumlamellen und vor allem immer wieder Glas – von den gläsernen Stützen im Rathaus von Saint-Germain-en-Laye bis zum Glasdach der Louvre-Werkstätten – werden eingesetzt und ergeben nur aus ihrer Bearbeitung und Fügung heraus die gewünschte Wirkung.

Dieses Undogmatische und Direkte, das nie monoton oder austauschbar wirkt, ist es, was von den Arbeiten von Jérôme Brunet und Eric Saunier ausströmt und sie so sympathisch macht. Ungleichartigkeit, Individualität und ein gewisser Widerspruch in manchen Konzepten gehören bei ihnen wohl dazu. Da mag man es auch verzeihen, daß bei der Klinik in Palavas-les-Flots in den Bodenschienen der hölzernen Schiebetüren, die bei den Fassaden die vorderste Schicht bilden, immer ein wenig der Sand knirschen wird, der vom Strand herübergeweht kommt.

The central hall of the town hall in Saint-Germain-en-Laye

Die zentrale Halle im Rathaus von Saint-Germain-en-Laye

The elementary school is located only 250 metres from the Roman arena in the heart of the old town. It is a steel and glass building, untypical for its site in Nîmes, with an aluminium slat skin that vibrates heavily once the Mistral begins to blow.

The original "La Placette" school was built at the turn of the century. In the course of the extension, the old building was left untouched with the exception of its south facade. The new building has literally pushed itself in front of the old one. In its organisation, the building is extremely simple. An internal passage covered by a glass roof was inserted between the old and the new building parts. A small row of cast-iron columns, once part of the colonnade of the south facade, was preserved, but located now in the middle of the new corridor it is no longer structurally relevant. Given the limited dimensions of the site and the constraints resulting from the need to retain the open square to the south, there was no alternative but to build directly along the side of the existing school. On the inside, this resulted in an economical floor plan, with the rooms arranged on both sides of the corridors. The new, reinforced concrete structure is the same height as the old building, creating unusually high classrooms for today's standards.

The new south and east facades are made up of a glass wall hidden behind a sunscreen-curtain that has a very technoid feeling to it, composed of aluminium slats and set 60 cm in front of the glass wall. To the architects, the facade is a transcription of a huge Venetian blind. The shading elements can be pivoted on a central axis, creating a rich play of shadows. Only the parapets are fixed.

To the east, a tower-like block containing stairs, lifts, the caretaker's flat and the library was added. The ground floor, slightly lower than street level, includes a large multi-purpose auditorium. Classrooms are located on three levels above.

Elementary School, Nîmes

Die Grundschule liegt nur 250 Meter von der römischen Arena entfernt inmitten der Altstadt. Es handelt sich um einen für die Lage in Nîmes ungewöhnlichen Stahl-Glas-Bau, dessen Lamellenhaut aus Aluminium beim Mistral heftig zu vibrieren beginnt.

Die Schule „La Placette" entstand um die Jahrhundertwende und ist bei der Erweiterung durch Brunet und Saunier mit Ausnahme der Südfassade erhalten geblieben. Der Neubau hat sich regelrecht davorgeschoben. Er besteht aus einem extrem einfach aufgebauten Gebäuderiegel. Zwischen Alt- und Neubau wurde ein interner Glasdach-Gang eingefügt. Die kleine Reihe gußeiserner Säulen, die zu den Kolonnaden der alten Südfassade gehörten, blieb erhalten, hat aber, in der Mitte des Flurs stehend, keine konstruktive Bedeutung mehr. Das knapp bemessene Terrain ließ unter Beibehaltung eines größeren Platzraumes im Süden kein anderes Konzept zu als den direkten Anbau an die Flanke des Altbaus. Innen konnte mit diesem Konzept eine zweibündige Anlage mit guter Ausnutzung realisiert werden. Die Stahlbetonkonstruktion des neuen Gebäudeflügels nimmt die Höhen des Altbaus auf. Dadurch ergeben sich für heutige Verhältnisse ungewöhnlich hohe Klassenräume.

Die neue Süd- und Ostfassade besteht aus einer Glaswand, die von einem sehr technoid wirkenden Sonnenschutz-Vorhang aus Aluminiumlamellen, der 60 cm vor dem Baukörper liegt, verdeckt ist. Für die Architekten stellt sie eine Transkription einer riesigen Jalousie dar. Die Sonnenschutzelemente lassen sich um eine vertikale Achse drehen und sorgen für ein reiches Schattenspiel. Nur die Brüstungsfelder sind fest installiert.

Östlich des Neu- und Altbaus ist ein turmartiger Block angefügt, der die Treppen, Aufzüge sowie die Hausmeisterwohnung und die Bibliothek aufnimmt. Das leicht

The roof, partially spread with artificial lawn, constitutes the play area for the older children, whose classrooms are located on the floor below. An umbrella-structure tensioned by steel cables, meant to recall the large tent roofs that once protected the stands of the Roman arenas, covers the roof of the new building.

The triangular play area in front of the new building is remarkable as it opens the school toward the city. Children are not locked away in a courtyard, but can play within the urban environment, and yet they are removed from the square by the difference in level. The adjoining church frames the square to the east. Despite the new building it remains the dominant structure here.

unter Straßenniveau liegende Erdgeschoß des Neubaus nimmt den großen Mehrzwecksaal auf. Darüber sind auf drei Geschossen die Klassenräume angeordnet. Auf dem Dach liegt eine teilweise mit Kunstrasen ausgelegte Pausenfläche für die älteren Kinder, die ihre Klassenräume im 3. Obergeschoß haben. Sie wird beim Neubau mit einem durch Stahltrosse verspannten Dachschirm überdeckt. Er soll an die großen Zeltdächer erinnern, die die Tribünen der römischen Arenen vor der Sonne schützten.

Außergewöhnlich ist der dem Neubau vorgelagerte dreieckige Pausenhof. Die Schule öffnet sich damit zur Stadt, die Kinder spielen nicht abgeschlossen in einem Hof, sondern in der Stadt und sind durch die Höhendifferenz dennoch vom Platz abgesetzt. Die angrenzende Kirche bildet die Platzkante im Osten. Sie bleibt trotz des Neubaus der dominierende Bau am Ort.

The sunscreen-curtain to the square is made up of aluminium slats. Gigantic loggias were punched into the first and second storeys.

Der Sonnenschutz-Vorhang zum Platz besteht aus Aluminiumlamellen. Im ersten und zweiten Obergeschoß wurden riesige Loggien ausgespart.

The break area for older
children is located on the
roof under a rigged white
canvas structure

Der Pausenhof für die
größeren Kinder befindet
sich auf dem Dach unter
einer verspannten Kon-
struktion aus weißen
Planen

The "schoolyard" is a large
loggia on the buildings
second floor

Als große Loggia
integrierter „Pausenhof"
im 2. Obergeschoß

The western front side
with fire-escape and
existing building to the left

Die westliche Stirnseite mit
Fluchttreppenhaus. Links
der Altbau

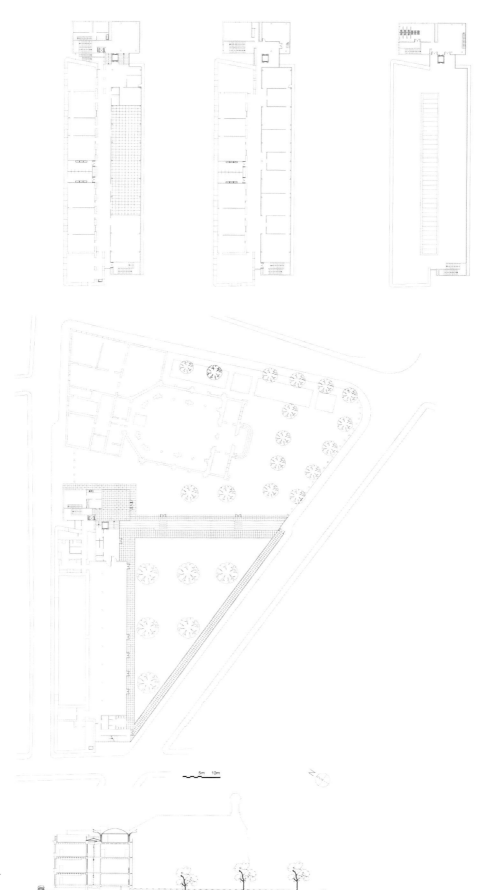

Ground floor, first, third
and roof floor plans and
section

Grundrisse Erdgeschoß,
erstes und drittes Obergeschoß, Dachgeschoß und
Schnitt

Over the past fifteen years, numerous architects besides Ieoh Ming Pei have been commissioned with new buildings and building alterations in various parts of the Grand Louvre. Brunet and Saunier's project remains almost entirely hidden. The difficult, compromised task consisted in relocating research laboratories for the conservation and documentation of objects of art, founded in 1931, to a large, new, three-level basement. Approximately 1500 pieces of art are examined and classified here each year by scientists and restorers of the French museums. What leeway was there? The architects were well aware that the experts' previous workplace had been at roof level of the Pavillon de Flore at the southern end of the Louvre, commanding spectacular views of the Louvre and the city. These people were about to be relocated to spaces up to 12 metres below ground beneath the Jardin du Caroussel. They had to be presented with something quite unusual.

The concept is simple. A continuous glass skin connects the three subterranean levels across their entire height to a central atrium. Bridges on the upper floors connect the two sides. The hall-like space, only 4 metres wide, is covered by a glass roof 16 metres long at the level of the Jardin du Caroussel. It is made up of separate vertical glass elements that project the captured light downward like prisms. The glass roof slopes at 3% and to the pedestrian looks like a reflecting surface of water framed by a planted border.

The central play of light is not enough to light the rooms, but it establishes the crucial visual connection to the sky. The central space with its spot-fixed glass walls, which demanded great transparency within the different parts of the workshops, has created a new type of spatial quality, characterized by spaciousness

Louvre Research Laboratories, Paris

Section through the research laboratories below the Jardin du Caroussel at the south wing of the Grand Louvre

Schnitt durch die Forschungswerkstätten unterhalb des Jardin du Caroussel am Südflügel des Grand Louvre

Neben Ieoh Ming Pei haben in den letzten fünfzehn Jahren zahlreiche andere Architekten in unterschiedlichen Bereichen des Grand Louvre Neu- und Umbauten vorgenommen. Das Projekt von Brunet und Saunier bleibt nahezu vollständig im Verborgenen. Ihre schwierige, mit Kompromissen behaftete Aufgabe bestand darin, in einem neuen großen Souterrain auf drei Geschossen die 1931 gegründeten Forschungswerkstätten der Konservierung und Dokumentation von Exponaten unterzubringen. Jährlich werden hier von Wissenschaftlern und Restauratoren der französischen Museen rund 1500 Kunstobjekte untersucht und klassifiziert.

Welche Spielräume gab es? Die Architekten wußten, daß die dort Tätigen zuvor im Dachgeschoß des Pavillon de Flore am Ende des südlichen Louvre-Flügels mit schönsten Ausblicken auf den Louvre und die Stadt gearbeitet hatten und nun sozusagen im Untergrund des Jardin du Caroussel in einer Tiefe von bis zu 12 Metern ihre Räume finden sollten. Ihnen mußte daher etwas geboten werden. Das Konzept ist einfach: Die drei unterirdischen Ebenen öffnen sich mit einer durchgehenden Glashaut auf einen die gesamte Höhe einnehmenden zentralen, in etwa mittig angeordneten Lichthof. Passerellen stellen bei den oberen Ebenen die Verbindung zwischen den zwei Bereichen her. Der nur 4 Meter breite hallenartige Raum wird auf dem Niveau des Jardin du Caroussel durch ein 16 Meter langes, einzigartig konzipiertes Glasdach abgeschlossen. Es handelt sich um einzelne vertikale Schotten, die wie Prismen das von der gläsernen Oberfläche eingefangene Licht in die Tiefe projizieren. Das Glasdach mit einem Gefälle von 3 % erscheint dem Passanten wie eine sich spiegelnde Wasserfläche, die von einem „Brunnenrand" mit Grünzone umgeben ist.

Das zentrale Lichtspiel reicht zwar nicht für die Belichtung der Räume aus, sorgt

The three levels of laboratories are lit exclusively by a central skylight

Die dreigeschossigen Werkstätten werden ausschließlich über ein zentrales Oberlicht belichtet

The glass roof above the courtyard is self-bearing with its glass joists

Das Glasdach über dem Lichthof trägt sich mit seinen gläsernen Schotten selbst

that almost makes one forget the absent views. To the architects, the result is a metaphorical, in some ways a religious place, where the path from darkness to light has a mysterious quality.

Entering light encounters no obstruction. Neither the glass roof nor the workshop walls include structural elements not made of glass. The roof is self-supported by the glass elements that are 4.60 m long and 60 cm high, consist of four layers of glass, each 1.5 cm thick, and function as joists. Walls are designed as structural skins. Glass is not simply inserted, it is transformed into an integral structural element – used in this way for the first time in France.

aber immerhin für den wichtigen Sichtbezug zum Himmel. Durch den zentralen Raum mit den punktförmig gehaltenen Glaswänden, der eine große Transparenz innerhalb der einzelnen Teile der Werkstätten voraussetzte, ergab sich eine neue, von Großzügigkeit geprägte Raumqualität, die die mangelnden Ausblicke fast vergessen läßt. Für die Architekten ist ein metaphorischer, gewissermaßen auch religiöser Ort entstanden, bei dem der Weg von der Dunkelheit und Verborgenheit zum Licht etwas Geheimnisvolles hat.

Das Licht hat keine Hindernisse zu überwinden. Weder das gläserne Flachdach noch die Wände der Werkstätten weisen Konstruktionselemente auf. Das Dach trägt sich durch die 4,60 Meter langen und 60 Zentimeter hohen gläsernen Schotten selbst. Aus vier jeweils 1,5 Zentimeter dicken Schichten bestehend, fungieren sie als Unterzüge. Die Wände sind freitragend als Haut konzipiert. Das Glas wird nicht eingefügt, sondern zu einem integralen konstruktiven Bestandteil transformiert – in dieser Form zum erstenmal in Frankreich.

The street facade is characterized by powerful vertical divisions and an entrance area that swings inward in a concave curve

Die Straßenfassade wird von mächtigen Schotten und einem konkav eingeschwungenen Eingangsbereich bestimmt

Partial view of the facade facing the cemetery

Ausschnitt der Fassade zum Friedhof

The square roof of the hall with its central atrium is surrounded by two floors of offices

Das quadratische Hallendach mit zentralem Atrium ist von zwei Bürogeschossen umgeben

The central hall is entirely covered by a glass roof supported by twelve cross-shaped glass columns

Die zentrale Halle wurde komplett mit einem gläsernen Dach versehen, das von zwölf gläsernen Kreuzstützen getragen wird

Plans of ground and
upper floors and elevation
on Rue Léon-Désoyer

Grundrisse Erd- und
Obergeschosse sowie
Ansicht von der Rue
Léon-Désoyer

The secondary school of Rozay-en-Brie in the Département Seine-et-Marne resembles a small cité in its own right, located between a new residential neighbourhood and a supermarket. With its calm and easily legible exterior, the building is decisively set apart from its surroundings. With its "urban spaces", it is clearly organised and has an obvious hierarchy, manifest, for instance, in the enclosed square as the central space and the open galleries for circulation. In terms of typology, a certain relation to the large farm estates of the region can be made out. The closed-off character of these estates, however, is superceded by great transparency here.

The main building is made up of a low square block, laid out like a cloister in its basic organisation. An axial walk traverses the school in a north-south direction and continues in the outdoors. To date, only the first building phase has been completed, so that the school is currently U-shaped in plan and the architects' conceptual idea cannot be experienced.

The totally glazed facades are a special feature, creating transparency even across the large interior courtyard. The architects managed to establish a relationship between the school and its surroundings that dissolves any feeling of being locked in. Glass is used in different ways: clear glass in the classrooms; large formats, as in storefronts, in the large hall and the cafeteria; serigraphed and opaque glass in rooms where visual connections are not, or only partially, desired. The open facades project great lightness.

This lightness is also expressed in other ways. The building itself seems unconnected to the ground, poised there "like a leaf". Wooden floors and undersides of roofs are made of tropical Iroko wood.

Secondary School, Rozay-en-Brie

Die Oberschule von Rozay-en-Brie im Département Seine-et-Marne zeigt sich zwischen Neubauviertel und Supermarkt als eine kleine eigenständige Cité. Der Bau hebt sich mit seinem ruhigen und leicht ablesbaren Äußeren entschieden von seiner Umgebung ab. Er ist mit seinen „urbanen Räumen" klar konzipiert und hierarchisiert. Dazu gehören der umschlossene Platz als Mittelpunkt und die offenen Galerien als Wege. Typologisch ist eine gewisse Ähnlichkeit zu den großen Gutshöfen in der Region erkennbar. Die äußere Geschlossenheit dieser Höfe weicht hier jedoch einer großen Transparenz.

Das Hauptgebäude besteht aus einem flachen quadratischen Block, der in seiner Grundstruktur wie ein Kreuzgang konzipiert ist. Eine axiale Nord-Süd-Wegebeziehung führt durch die Schule und setzt sich im Außenbereich fort. Bisher wurde nur der erste Bauabschnitt realisiert, so daß die Schule eine U-förmige Grundstruktur aufweist. Die konzeptionelle Idee der Architekten ist daher zur Zeit im Ganzen nicht erfahrbar.

Eine Besonderheit sind die vollständig verglasten Fassaden, die auch für eine Transparenz über den großen internen Hof hinweg sorgen. Den Architekten ist es hier gelungen, eine Beziehung zwischen Schule und Umgebung zu schaffen, die jedes Gefühl von Eingesperrtsein verwischt.

Das Glas fand in unterschiedlicher Form Verwendung: Klarglas für die Klassenräume, zum Teil großformatig wie Schaufenster für die große Halle und das Schulrestaurant; serigrafiertes Glas und opakes Glas für weitere Räume, wo der Ein- und Ausblick nicht oder nur zum Teil gewünscht ist. Die offenen Fassaden strahlen große Leichtigkeit aus.

Diese Leichtigkeit kommt auch in anderer Form zum Ausdruck. Das Gebäude scheint nicht mit dem Boden verhaftet zu sein. Man hat eher den Eindruck, daß

The school is located on the edge of town and is present as a glass hall with surrounding walkways

Die Schule steht am Ortsrand und zeigt sich als Glashalle mit Umgang

In the centre of the school's square figure there is a further, smaller building. It is the student house. Here the students have there "own" cafeteria and club room independent of the school. Two towering foreign-looking volumes appear to harbour secretive activities – one is totally closed, the other has a large window facing north. These are the school's music and art rooms.

The auditorium is inserted into the large hall as a slightly slanted block, trapezoidal in plan – an enigmatic "suitcase" enclosed by 600 student lockers. The contrast of opening and closure, a recurring motif of this school building, can be vividly experienced by the students.

es nur „wie ein Laubblatt" aufliegt. Für die hölzernen Böden und Dachuntersichten fand das Tropenholz Iroko Verwendung.

In der Mitte der quadratischen Figur der Schule steht ein weiteres, kleineres Gebäude. Es ist das Schülerhaus. Unabhängig vom Schulbau sind hier die „eigene" Cafeteria und der Klubraum untergebracht. Zwei emporragende, in ihrem Äußeren fremd wirkende Volumen lassen Geheimnisvolles vermuten – das eine ist völlig verschlossen, das andere verfügt über ein großes Nordlicht-Fenster: Es sind der Musik- und der Zeichensaal der Schule.

In der großen Halle ist die Aula als leicht geneigter Block auf trapezförmigem Grundriß eingestellt – ein enigmatischer „Koffer", der von den 600 Schließfächern der Schüler ummantelt ist. Offenheit und Geschlossenheit werden bei dieser Schule spannungsvoll und für die Schüler unmittelbar erfahrbar gegenübergestellt.

The roof with a wooden underside is supported by slender round columns

Das Dach mit hölzerner Unteransicht wird mit schlanken Rundstützen abgefangen

82

School and concert hall are
two clearly separate building parts

Bei dem Bau setzen sich
die Schule und der Konzertsaal deutlich voneinander
ab

Side facade with
concert hall

Seitenansicht mit dem
Konzertsaal

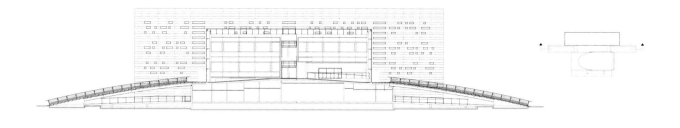

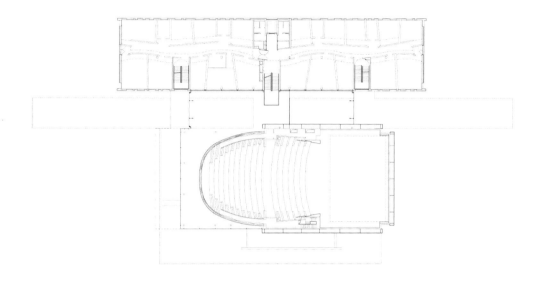

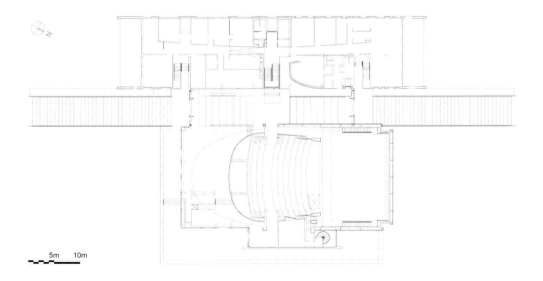

5m   10m

The central hall
separates the building
parts. Floor plans and
sections

Die zentrale Halle
trennt die Gebäude-
teile. Grundrisse und
Schnitte

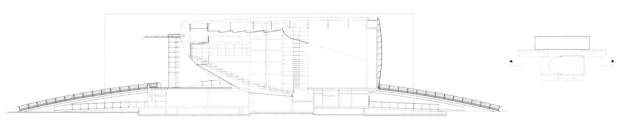

91

The site of the Montpellier branch of the Banque de France is located on a winding street in an old residential suburb on the slightly elevated edge of town, characterized by a remarkable population of trees. The building is set back from the street and composed of three interlocking volumes that look out onto different parts of the garden.

The most important section of the Banque de France is the vault where large quantities of money are temporarily stored. This highly secured zone is located in the plinth of the building and is accessed by money transporters from the east. The vehicles pass an additional control point erected on the border of the property and then descend a ramp down to a lock.

The highest part of the building complex is a glazed slab, placed at right angles to the street. It contains two levels of offices laid out on both sides of the corridors. The northern end of the upper floor forms a terrace for the conference room and the director's office. From this higher building part, staff have a view east over the roof of the lower, main building volume, planked with tropical wood. The roof is not accessible.

The main building volume contains the large, light-flooded lobby. Visitors arriving from the client parking area to the south are lavishly welcomed. Here, in particular, at the entrance to the lobby, the architects' model – Ludwig Mies van der Rohe's Barcelona Pavilion – is unmistakably present. Set on a stone plinth along the long side of the facade, here clad in steel plate, two white round columns lead visitors through the security lock placed at right angles to the facade. An enormous steel beam marks the edge of the projecting roof. Until they reach

Banque de France, Montpellier

Das Grundstück der Niederlassung der Banque de France in Montpellier befindet sich an einer kurvigen Straße in einem alten, von außergewöhnlichem Baumbestand geprägten Villenviertel am leicht erhöht gelegenen Stadtrand. Der von der Straße zurückgesetzte Bau ist aus drei ineinander verschachtelten Gebäudekuben zusammengefügt, die sich zu unterschiedlich gestalteten Gartenzonen öffnen.

Der wichtigste Bereich der Banque de France ist der Tresorraum, wo große Mengen Geld zwischengelagert werden müssen. Diese besonders gesicherte Zone des Gebäudes liegt im Sockelgeschoß und wird mit den Geldtransportern im Osten erreicht. Die Fahrzeuge müssen eine zusätzliche Kontrollstation passieren, die an der Grundstückskante errichtet wurde, und fahren anschließend eine Rampe hinunter zur Schleuse.

In dem von der Straße her gesehen quer auf dem Grundstück stehenden höchsten Teil des Gebäudekomplexes, dem verglasten Riegel, befinden sich auf zwei Ebenen zweibündige Bürotrakte. Der nördliche Abschluß des oberen Geschosses ist als Terrasse für den Sitzungssaal und das Büro des Bankdirektors ausgebildet. Von diesem höheren Bauteil blicken die Mitarbeiter nach Osten auf die mit Tropenholz beplankte Dachfläche des flacheren Hauptbaukörpers, die allerdings nicht zugänglich ist.

Der Hauptbau beherbergt in erster Linie die große, lichtdurchflutete Empfangshalle. Der Besucher, der vom Kundenparkplatz im Süden kommt, wird großzügig empfangen. Besonders hier, am Entree in die Halle, ist das Leitbild der Architekten – der Barcelona-Pavillon von Ludwig Mies van der Rohe – unverkennbar gegenwärtig. Über einem hellen steinernen Sockel längs der Fassade, die hier mit Stahlplatten verkleidet ist, leiten zwei weiße Rundstützen den Besucher durch

At the entrance, the Barcelona Pavilion as the building's model is unmistakable

Besonders am Eingang ist das Leitbild Barcelona-Pavillon unverkennbar

the security lock, visitors are likely to feel that they are about to enter an art collection. Inside, an extensive circulation zone with waiting areas is located to the left, while the banking hall lies to the right. This space is well-lit through the long facades, also at the back, where employees work on a slightly elevated level. With this astute concept, the architects succeeded in articulating the open office wing. Light is also admitted through a narrow slit in the roof and a glass spiral stair leading up to the office wing.

Functionally separate but integrated in terms of mass, the third building volume includes the restaurant and a terrace extending to the north. From here there is a beautiful view of the sloping terrain with

die quer zur Fassade vorgeschobene Schleuse. Ein mächtiger Stahlträger markiert die Kante des großen Vordachs. Bis zu dieser Schleuse hat der Besucher eher den Eindruck, sich am Zugang einer Ausstellungshalle einer Kunstsammlung zu befinden. Hinter dem Eingang liegen links der weiträumige Erschließungsbereich mit Wartezonen und rechts die Schalterhalle. Sie erhält viel Licht über die langen Fassaden auch auf der Rückseite, wo die Angestellten auf einer leicht erhöhten Ebene arbeiten. Mit diesem geschickten Konzept gelingt es, den offenen Bürotrakt abzuheben. Licht kommt zusätzlich über eine schmale Spalte im Dach und durch eine gläserne Wendeltreppe, die zum Bürotrakt hinaufführt.

Funktional getrennt, aber als Baukörper integriert, schließt sich der dritte Gebäudeteil mit Restaurant und einer im Norden vorgelagerten Terrasse an. Geboten wird hier ein schöner Ausblick in das leicht abfallende, dicht bewachsene Terrain und auf den au-

The banking hall is glazed
on both sides and charac-
terised by its sober ele-
gance

Die Schalterhalle ist beid-
seitig verglast und strahlt
nüchterne Eleganz aus

its dense vegetation and the extraordinary trees of
the neighbouring property. A bar within the main
building is delicately partitioned from the banking
hall and the circulation zone by opaque glass. The
bar creates the transition to an auditorium beneath
the office wing. The mandatory offices of the different labour unions are located behind the restaurant.
The Banque de France building owes its force to the
materials, the transparency and the exciting concept
of different levels with distinct uses. The dialogue
continues in the relation of interior and exterior and
takes advantage of the park-like surroundings.

ßergewöhnlichen Baumbestand des Nachbargrund-
stücks. Noch im Hauptgebäude gibt es eine vom Erschließungsbereich und der Schalterhalle durch
Opakglas leicht abgesetzte Bar. Sie bildet den Über-
gang zu einem unter dem Bürotrakt gelegenen Ver-
anstaltungssaal. Hinter dem Restaurant befinden
sich die obligatorischen Büroräume für die verschiedenen Gewerkschaften.

Das Gebäude der Banque de France lebt von den
Materialien, der Transparenz und von der spannungsvollen Konzeption der verschiedenen Ebenen
mit den unterschiedlichen Nutzungen. Dieser Dialog setzt sich beim Bezug von innen und außen fort,
der durch die parkartige Anlage profitiert.

Two views of the wooden
walkways that wrap around
the office wing

Zwei Blicke auf die hölzernen Umgänge am Büro-
trakt

Terrace of the staff recrea-
tion area

Terrasse des Pausenbe-
reichs der Mitarbeiter

View from the west of the
building's back section
with conference halls on
the ground floor

Blick von Westen auf den
hinteren Gebäuderiegel. Im
Erdgeschoß befinden sich
Versammlungsräume

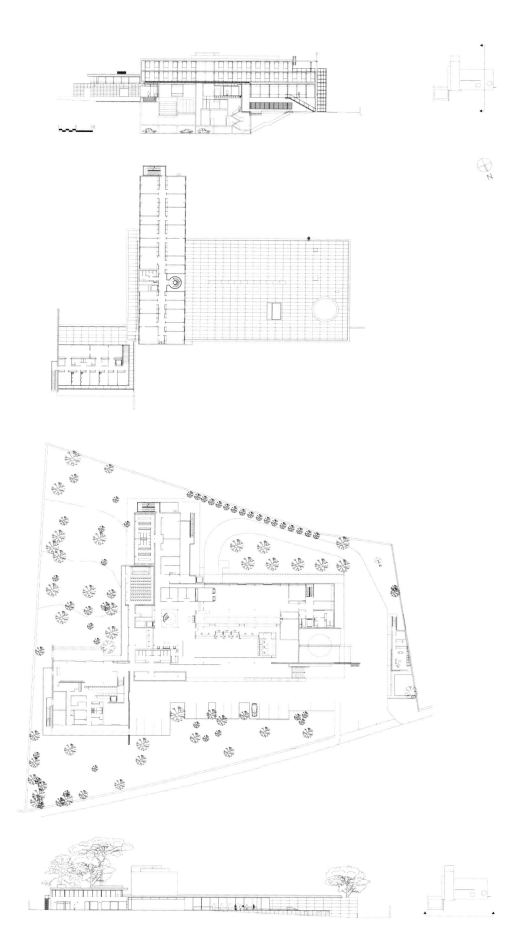

Section, ground and upper
floor plans and elevation

Schnitt, Grundrisse Erd-
und Obergeschoß und
Ansicht

Saint-Pierre Institute in Palavas-les-Flots, a small resort town on the Mediterranean south of Montpellier, is a private rehabilitation clinic for children. It has a long and eventful history. After modest beginnings in huts on the beach, in the twenties the donation of a large piece of property enabled the construction of a three-storey building with dormitories, examination rooms, a refectory and a chapel. After several extensions, the building finally reached a total length of 240 metres.

Planning a new clinic became necessary as the old complex no longer complied with today's requirements in terms of space and technology. With the support of a general contractor, an ideas competition was organised among five architecture practices and a decision was quickly made. After only four years of planning and construction, the clinic was inaugurated in April 1999.

The complex is made up of a two-storey yellow building volume along the road, a lower connecting zone, and a four-storey building volume, rendered in an ox-blood colour, almost U-shaped in plan and open to the south toward the sea. Its concrete floor slabs project to shade the floors below. The first, slanted, view from the street leaves visitors with an unclear impression of several different building volumes.

Arriving visitors step between the buildings on to a creaking area planked with tropical Ipé wood and screened by a low pergola. The columns with cross sections, whose profiles broaden slightly upward, are set in a square grid and are anchored with steel "shoes". This peaceful, almost cosy "anteroom" generates a feeling of being protected and well taken care of. The wooden arrival area deliberately makes no reference to a sanatorium and is – free of any daintiness – a space for children.

Saint-Pierre Institute, Palavas-les-Flots

Das Institut Saint-Pierre in Palavas-les-Flots, einem kleinen Badeort südlich von Montpellier am Mittelmeer, ist eine private Rehabilitationseinrichtung für Kinder. Sie hat eine lange und bewegte Geschichte. Nach bescheidenen Anfängen in Hütten am Strand gelang durch die Schenkung eines großen Grundstücks in den zwanziger Jahren der Bau eines dreigeschossigen Gebäudes mit Schlafsälen, Untersuchungsräumen, Refektorium und Kapelle. Dieser Bau erreichte nach Erweiterungen eine Länge von 240 Metern.

Eine Neuplanung der Klinik wurde erforderlich, da der alte Gebäudekomplex heutigen Standards hinsichtlich der Raumzuordnung und der Technik nicht mehr entsprach. Mit der Unterstützung eines Generalübernehmers wurde nach einem Ideenwettbewerb unter fünf Architekturbüros sehr schnell entschieden. Innerhalb von nur vier Jahren Planung und Bau konnte die Klinik im April 1999 bezogen werden.

Der Komplex setzt sich aus einem zweigeschossigen gelbfarbenen Gebäuderiegel entlang der Straße, einer niedrigen Zwischenzone und einem nahezu U-förmigen viergeschossigen Gebäudeteil zusammen, der sich nach Süden zum Meer öffnet. Er ist ochsenblutfarben verputzt. Die einzelnen Geschoßebenen treten bei diesem Gebäudeteil durch vorkragende Betonebenen hervor, die für Verschattung sorgen. Die Schrägansicht von der Straße bietet dem Ankommenden zunächst ein etwas undefiniertes Bild unterschiedlicher Gebäude.

Der Besucher tritt zwischen den Gebäuden in eine mit dem Tropenholz Ipé beplankte, leicht knarrende Zone, die durch eine niedrige Pergola abgeschirmt ist. Die kreuzförmig ausgebildeten Stützen, deren Profile sich nach oben leicht verbreitern, stehen in einem Quadratraster und sind in stählernen „Schuhen" verankert. Man hat bei diesem beschaulichen, fast schon wohnlichen „Vorraum" un-

The building is located right on the beach and consists of a base with rehabilitation facilities and three floors of patient rooms

Das Gebäude steht direkt am Strand und setzt sich aus einem Sockel mit den Reha-Einrichtungen und drei Bettenebenen zusammen

Behind a sliding door, the actual entrance lobby is a glazed intermediate zone which opens west on to a green patio. It connects to doctors' rooms for external patients to the north, and leads to examination rooms to the south. To the west, the patio is bordered by an elevated café terrace reached across an open stair. The lobby is the central connecting space to the south, culminating on the beach in a courtyard of palm trees.

The clinic's real charme, however, is experienced only on the upper levels. Three floors of patient rooms are terraced and oriented to the sea in a U-shape. The shorter wings contain patients' rooms of different sizes, while the central, set-back section includes the dining and play areas as well as the staff rooms. It was important to Brunet and Saunier that the children be screened from their neighbours, and yet, being accomodated right on the water, that they have maximum open space directly in front of their rooms. The first floor of the patient wing is the most generous. The windows open on to a terrace with a pergola-covered walk along the sea. From here it is possible to look down into the two courtyards planted with palm trees that flank the sea-front therapy pool hall.

mittelbar den Eindruck, gut aufgehoben und bestens umsorgt zu sein. Dieser hölzerne Vorbereich stellt ganz bewußt keinen Bezug zu einer Heilanstalt her und ist eher – ohne jede Verspieltheit – ein Raum für Kinder.

Beim eigentlichen Entree hinter einer Schiebetür handelt es sich um eine verglaste Zwischenzone, die sich nach Westen zu einem begrünten Patio öffnet. Nördlich schließen Arzträume für externe Patienten an. Südlich befinden sich Untersuchungsräume. Den westlichen Abschluß des Patios bildet eine Café-Terrasse, zu der eine offene Treppe hinaufführt. Das Entree stellt nach Süden den zentralen Verbindungsraum her, der am Strand in einem Palmenhof endet. Der eigentliche Reiz des Klinikgebäudes wird erst in den Obergeschossen erfahrbar, wo sich die drei Ebenen des Bettentrakts nahezu U-förmig zum Meer öffnen und dabei zurückgetreppt angelegt sind. In den Querflügeln befinden sich die unterschiedlich großen Krankenzimmer, während der mittlere, zurückliegende Teil als Eß- und Spielzone dient und außerdem die Räume des Pflegepersonals beherbergt. Brunet und Saunier war es wichtig, daß den Kindern – weitgehend abgeschirmt von der Nachbarschaft und dennoch direkt am Meer – größtmögliche Freibereiche

The terraced patient wing opens to the sea almost U-shaped in plan

Der Bettentrakt öffnet sich nahezu u-förmig zum Meer und treppt sich dabei zurück

Seen from the sea, the long building is extraordinarily elegant. Except for two openings leading to the courtyards, the ground floor consists of a wall of wooden slats that forms a closed surface set in front of the actual building. People behind the wall are discerned as outlines only. The two entrance openings can be shut with sliding doors made of the same wooden slats, so that the pool can be entirely closed to the outside, especially during the busy beach season. The palm trees will grow higher than the wooden wall in the course of time.

vor den Zimmern zur Verfügung stehen. Das erste Obergeschoß dieses Bettentrakts ist am großzügigsten konzipiert. Hier öffnen sich die Zimmer auf eine vorgelagerte Terrasse, die längs zum Meer eine mit Pergola überdachte Passage aufweist. Man kann hinunterblicken in die zwei Palmenhöfe, zwischen denen sich zum Strand hin die Halle mit dem Therapiebecken befindet.

Vom Meer aus zeigt sich das langgezogene Haus von außerordentlicher Eleganz. Das Erdgeschoß besteht – mit Ausnahme der Eingänge in die zwei Zwischenhöfe – aus einer vorgestellten Holzlamellen-Wand, die eine geschlossene Fläche bildet. Hinter dieser sind Personen schemenhaft zu erkennen. Auch die beiden Zugänge lassen sich durch Lamellenholz-Rollentore schließen, so daß vor allem während der Hochsaison die völlige Abschottung vom Badebetrieb gewährleistet ist. Die Palmen der Höfe sollen einmal über die Lamellenwand hinauswachsen.

The individual patient rooms can be closed with sliding doors made of wooden slats

Die einzelnen Krankenzimmer können durch die hölzernen Lamellen-Rollentore verschlossen werden

The terraces in front of the building and the pergola on the first floor are reminiscent of a ship's deck

Die vorgelagerten Terrassen und die Pergola im ersten Obergeschoß lassen ein wenig an ein Schiffsdeck denken

The therapy rooms on the ground floor enclose two courtyards with palm trees with direct access to the sea

Die Therapieräume im Erdgeschoß umgeben zwei Palmenhöfe, die einen Zugang zum Meer bieten

The residential block uses glass as its most prominent feature. Positioned at right angles to the Seine on Rue Neuve Tolbiac, it faces an old cold-storage depot, one of the few original buildings remaining in "Seine Rive Gauche". Surrounding the four towers of Dominique Perrault's Bibliothèque Nationale, this important urban redevelopent area is more than three kilometres long and includes 130 hectares of land. According to the design guidelines for the entire area approved in 1989, floors are terraced toward the Seine. Thus the two top floors have enormous roof terraces. The orthogonal building volume with its three slightly projecting extensions toward the block interior were also stipulated in the design brief.

Although the project is subsidised social housing, the architectural language and its location next to the Bibliothèque Nationale suggest luxury condominiums. Despite size limits and other norms, the architects managed to develop simple spatial solutions for the 95 flats, remarkable in particular because of good functional relationships. Nevertheless, despite some open spatial sequences in the flats, in many cases their layout is unaccustomed and cornered. Clearly, the architects designed a building influenced by the rational simplicity and legibility of housing blocks of the seventies. This is apparent above all in the orthogonal floor plans, the balconies and the large glass sliding doors.

The building is strongly characterised by the continuous horizontal bands of balconies. This clarity and generous scale is maintained in the lobbies that span the entire depth of the building. In order to comply with the vertical facade rhythm required by the design guidelines, the duplex flats above the entrances were slighty set back to create structuring incisions. The organisation of the

Residential Building Rue Neuve Tolbiac, Paris

Der weitgehend gläserne Wohnblock steht quer zur Seine an der Rue Neuve Tolbiac. Er bildet das Gegenüber zu einem alten Kühlhaus, einem der wenigen Altbauten im „Seine Rive Gauche", dem mit 130 Hektar auf 3 Kilometern Länge bedeutenden Stadtentwicklungsgebiet im Südwesten von Paris, das die vier Türme der Bibliothèque Nationale von Dominique Perrault umgibt. Entsprechend den Gestaltungsrichtlinien von 1989, die für das gesamte Quartier festgelegt wurden, treppen sich die Geschosse zur Seine hin ab. Dadurch verfügen die zwei obersten Ebenen über riesige Dachterrassen. Auch die orthogonale Kubatur mit drei leicht vorspringenden Erweiterungen zum Blockinneren hin folgt präzis den Vorgaben.

Es handelt sich bei diesem Projekt um staatlich geförderten Wohnungsbau, der hier in einer architektonischen Sprache gelang, die an diesem Standort, neben der Bibliothèque Nationale, eher Luxuswohnungen vermuten lassen würde. Für die Räume der 95 Wohnungen konnten trotz der Festlegungen durch Flächenvorgaben und andere Normen einfache Lösungen erarbeitet werden, die sich vor allem durch gute funktionale Bezüge auszeichnen. Trotz der zum Teil offenen Raumfolgen bleibt die Aufteilung der Wohnungen jedoch häufig ungewohnt und allzu verwinkelt. Unverkennbar haben die Architekten hier einen Bau realisiert, der von der rationalen Einfachheit und Ablesbarkeit der Wohnblocks der siebziger Jahre geprägt ist. Dies zeigt sich vor allem an den rechtwinkligen Grundrissen, den Balkonen und den großen gläsernen Schiebetüren.

Der Bau wird stark von der Horizontalen der umlaufenden Balkonbänder geprägt. Diese Klarheit und Großzügigkeit setzt sich in den die gesamte Tiefe des Gebäudes einnehmenden Eingangshallen fort. Um auch der ebenfalls vorgegebenen vertikalen Rhythmik bei den Fassaden Genüge zu tun, treten die über den Eingän-

The largely glazed building is characterised by continuous bands of balconies with black type. Dominique Perrault's Bibliothèque nationale de France in the background

Der weitgehend gläserne Bau wird durch die umlaufenden Balkonbänder mit Schriftbildern geprägt. Im Hintergrund die Bibliothèque nationale de France von Dominique Perrault

building therefore becomes legible in the flight of the glass balcony parapets where fragments of texts by Jean Anouilh and Pierre Choderlos de Laclos were serigraphically applied. A surrounding new road and one of the pedestrian paths that traverse the block were named after the writers. The form of the black lettering on the balcony parapets wants to recall the blacksmiths' shops once located in the area.

A special quality in the flats is produced by the long rows of room-high sliding doors, made possible by lowering the radiators into the floor along the window fronts. In spite of their small size, therefore, thanks to the windows and extraordinary views, the flats can generate the feeling of being part of a lavish staging.

gen angeordneten Maisonette-Wohnungen in der 85 Meter langen Straßenfassade etwas zurück, so daß dort gliedernde Einschnitte entstehen. So läßt sich der Gebäudeaufbau an der Flucht der gläseren Balkonbrüstungen ablesen. Auf ihnen sind serigraphisch Bruchstücke aus Texten der Schriftsteller Jean Anouilh und Pierre Choderlos de Laclos aufgebracht wurden. Eine umliegende neue Straße und einer der Wege, der durch den Block führt, sind nach ihnen benannt worden. Die Form der schwarzen Schriftzeichen an den Balkonbrüstungen soll an die früher hier ansässigen Eisenschmieden erinnern.

Für eine besondere Qualität der Wohnungen sorgen die langen Reihen raumhoher Schiebetüren, die dadurch realisiert werden konnten, daß die Heizkörper entlang der Fensterflächen in den Boden eingelassen wurden. Die Wohnungen atmen durch sie und die teilweise außergewöhnlichen Ausblicke trotz aller Flächenknappheit ein wenig den Geist einer großzügigen Inszenierung.

Rue de Flandre, near the Bassin de la Villette in the working-class 19th arrondissement, was widened on its north side in the sixties. Numerous turn-of-the-century buildings were demolished and replaced by high housing blocks, that only partially follow the line of the street. On its south side, a few large blocks, set back from the street, were added between the existing buildings. Because of the resulting discrepancies in scale, Rue de Flandre has assumed unusual urban form.

The new building is located at the northern end of Rue de Flandre, next to a train viaduct that crosses it here. Jérôme Brunet and Eric Saunier attempted to frame the corner block in a language unusual for their practice. In its size and homogeneity, the building acts like a counterweight to the large buildings in the street. Its facade structure, "classical" as the architects would say, is clearly based on the Parisian residential and office buildings of the 19th century.

The large French windows with white sliding shutters are not only components of the facade here, but added to form long rows they are its constituent elements. Vertically, the rows of shutters are interrupted only by the narrow bands of the floor slabs. The free alteration of open and closed surfaces dissolves the facade and even transforms it into a graphic system. In this sense, the facade is clearly set apart from its surroundings. It is an entirely original interpretation of the "Parisian house".

A debatable aspect of this building are the windows that cross floor height. The continuous floor bands outside do not correspond to the actual floor height on the inside. The upper glass zone of the windows, which masks the actual floor

Residential Buildings Rue de Flandre, Paris

Die Rue de Flandre nahe des Bassin de la Villette im populären 19. Arrondissement erfuhr in den sechziger Jahren an ihrer Nordseite eine Verbreiterung, für die zahlreiche Häuser der Jahrhundertwende abgebrochen und durch hohe Wohnblocks ersetzt wurden, die nur zum Teil der Straßenflucht folgen. Auf der Südseite wurden, von der Flucht zurückgesetzt, ein paar große Blocks zwischen Altbauten eingefügt. Die Straße hat mit diesen Maßstabssprüngen eine ungewöhnliche stadträumliche Gestalt angenommen.

Der Neubau steht am nördlichen Beginn der Rue de Flandre neben einer die Straße überquerenden Eisenbahnbrücke. Jérôme Brunet und Eric Saunier haben hier in einer für ihr Büro ungewöhnlichen Entwurfssprache versucht, den Eckblock neu zu fassen. Mit seiner Dimension und Einheitlichkeit bietet er den Großbauten an der Straße ein Gegenüber, zum anderen orientiert sich die von den Architekten als „klassisch" bezeichnete Fassadenstruktur unverkennbar an den Pariser Wohn- und Geschäftshäusern des 19. Jahrhunderts.

Die großen französischen Fenster mit ihren weißen Schiebe-Läden sind jedoch nicht nur Bestandteil der Fassade, sie selbst bilden, in langen Reihen nebeneinander gefügt, die Fassade. In der Vertikalen werden sie nur durch die schmalen Geschoßbänder unterbrochen. Der freie Wechsel von offenen und geschlossenen Flächen löst die Fassade auf und läßt sie sogar zu einem grafischen System werden. Die Fassade hebt sich bei näherer Betrachtung dann doch deutlich von der Umgebung ab. Sie bietet eine völlig eigenständige Interpretation des „Pariser Hauses".

Eine zumindest fragwürdige Idee stellt bei diesem Neubau die geschoßübergreifende Fenster-Konzeption dar. Die außen durchlaufenden Geschoßebenen entsprechen nicht der Höhe der inneren Decken. Die obere Glaszone, hinter der

The corner building is located at a prominent site next to a railway bridge at the northern end of Rue de Flandre

Das Eckgebäude steht an markanter Stelle neben einer Eisenbahnbrücke am nördlichen Beginn der Rue de Flandre

slab behind, is therefore made of dark mirrored glass. This is not, however, distinguishable as such from the outside. The horizontal band in the facade, then, is actually the parapet. As the parapet must be one metre high, it was necessary to add a pane of glass in front of the actual windows above. The actual window is still two metres high, and the clear height of the rooms measures 2.60 metres. But the generosity of the opening as celebrated in the facade is a fake. The building suggests historic proportions and is dishonest in doing so.

Including two garden buildings located along the railway tracks, a total of 55 flats were integrated into the block. One part of the ensemble along Rue de l'Argonne has not yet been built. The buildings are accessible along a footpath that extends across the full depth of the site. Open areas were designed by artist Jacqueline Dauriac.

sich die eigentliche Decke befindet, besteht daher aus dunklem Spiegelglas, das allerdings von außen als solches kaum auszumachen ist. Das horizontale Band in der Fassade ist als Brüstungsabschluß zu begreifen. Da die Brüstung eine Höhe von einem Meter aufweisen muß, wurde oberhalb dieses Streifens noch eine Glasscheibe vor die Fenster gesetzt. Das Fenster selbst hat immerhin noch eine Höhe von zwei Metern. Innen ergibt sich eine lichte Geschoßhöhe von 2.60 Metern. Die großzügige Öffnung, die in der Fassade zelebriert wird, ist aber dennoch nur vorgetäuscht. Damit suggeriert das Haus alte Proportionen und ist dabei nicht ehrlich.

Zusammen mit zwei Gartenhäusern entlang der Bahntrasse sind 55 Wohnungen in den Block integriert worden. Ein Bauabschnitt in der Rue de l'Argonne ist allerdings noch nicht realisiert. Die Erschließung erfolgt über einen Weg, der die gesamte Tiefe des Grundstücks einnimmt. Die Freibereiche hat die Künstlerin Jacqueline Dauriac gestaltet.

The facade language successfully creates a relation to the neighbouring buildings in the side street

Mit der Fassadensprache gelingt ein guter Anschluß an das Nachbargebäude in der Querstraße

Views of the back facade, very different from the front, with access galleries and terraces. Two low new buildings were also fit in here

Blicke auf die ganz anders gestaltete Hoffassade mit Laubengängen und Terrassen. Zwei niedrige Neubauten fanden hier noch Platz

The windows' upper glass zone, concealing the actual floor slab, is made of dark mirrored glass

Die obere Glaszone der Fenster, hinter der sich innen die eigentliche Decke befindet, besteht aus dunklem Spiegelglas

One of the duplex flats under the roof

Eine der Maisonette-Wohnungen auf dem Dach

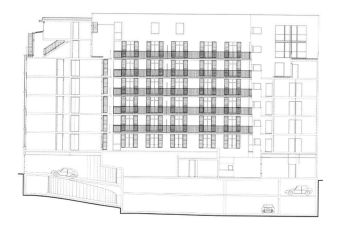
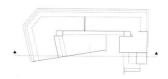

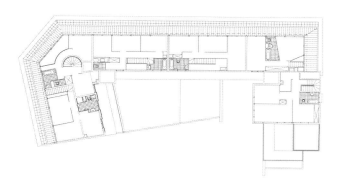

Floor plans and section
at courtyard

Grundrisse und Schnitt-
ansicht vom Hof

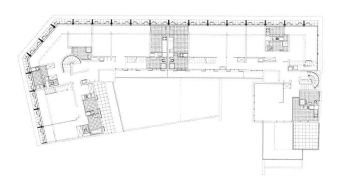

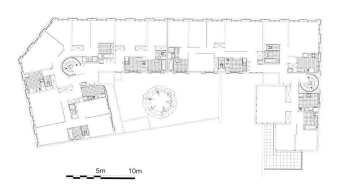

5m   10m

Agence Brunet/Saunier Paris

Biographies

Jérôme Brunet
Born 1954 – Gisors
École nationale supérieure des Beaux-Arts
1979 Diplôme d.p.l.g. UPA 7

Éric Saunier
Born 1952 – Paris
École nationale supérieure des Beaux-Arts
1980 Diplôme d.p.l.g. UPA 6

1981   Association Brunet/Saunier in Paris
1982   Laureates of the Young Architecture
          Albums
1991   Italstat Prize for Europe – mention

Benedictus Awards – mention
1994   Laboratoires de recherche des
          Musées de France à Paris
1996   Centre administratif de
          Saint-Germain-en-Laye

AMO Prize – nominated
1998   Siège régional de la Banque de
          France à Montpellier
2000   Institut Saint Pierre à Palavas-
          les-Flots

Selected Exhibitions

1982   Institut Français d'Architecture
          (IFA) – Paris, Pan XII
1983   Centre Beaubourg – Paris,
          Première œuvre
1987   Maison de l'Architecture – Paris,
          Un Maire – un architecte
1990   Institut Français d'Architecture
          (IFA) – Paris, 40 architectes de
          moins de 40 ans
1991   Centre Beaubourg – Paris,
          Constructions publiques
1994   Vienne, Paris, Londres, Berlin,
          Glasbau Seele
1997   Pavillon de l'Arsenal – Paris,
          Paris sous verre
1999   Bauhaus Universität – Weimar,
          Métamorphoses de l'espace au
          20ème siècle
2001   Berlin, Neue Räume

Members of Architecture Academy
Consulting members of *Mission Intermin-
istérielle pour la Qualité des Constructions
Publiques*

MUSEUM OF MUSIC Paris

ILOT DE LA STATION HOUSING Asnières

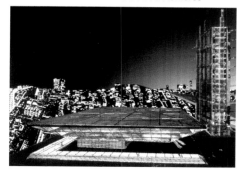

CULTURAL COMPLEX Alfortville

ECOLE NATIONALE SUPERIEURE DES TELECOM
Rue Vergniaud – rue Barrault, Paris 13th arrondissement
Competition – first prize
Two buildings to accomodate the administration and the council's hall, as well as training facilities
Client: Ministère des Postes et Télécommunications
Project leaders: Jean-Paul Roynette and Philippe Lair (competition), Vincent Marchand (studies and site)
Team: Daniel Guetta, Hervé Levaseux
Building technology: OTH Bâtiment
Value engineering: Ripeau
5 200 m² – completed 1991

1990

INTERCOMMUNAL HOSPITAL CENTRE
Avenue de Verdun, Créteil (Val-de-Marne)
Competition
Addition to the medical-technical block
Client: Centre Hospitalier
Project leader: Vincent Marchand
Team: Jean-Michel Reynier, Xavier Lagurgue, Clare Lasbrey, Thomas von Amelunxen
Building technology: OTH Bâtiments
Perspectives: Louis Paillard
13 000 m²

SEAT OF SOCIAL SERVICES LAFARGE-COPPEE
Rue des Belles Feuilles, Paris 16th arrondissement
Invited competition
Offices
Client: Kaufman & Broad
Project leader: Jean-Michel Reynier
Team: Sophie Nicolas, Thomas von Amelunxen, François Guidon
Perspectives: Didier Ghislain
Model: Eric Chicaez
6 500 m²

FRANCE ELECTRICITY (EDF) TRAINING CENTRE
Nanterre (Hauts-de-Seine)
Competition
Training facilities and workshops
Client: EDF
Team: Catherine Dormoy, Elisabeth Lemercier
Building technology: OTH Bâtiments
7 000 m²

MUSEUM OF MUSIC
Cité de la Musique, Paris 19th arrondissement
Competition
Museum layout
Client: Etablissement Public du Parc de la Villette

Project leader: Catherine Dormoy
Lighting: L'Observatoire 1- Georges Berne
Design of special uses of glass: Guillaume Saalburg
Building technology: Bethac – Value engineering: Ripeau
Perspectives: Vincent Lafont
4 500 m²

ILOT DE LA STATION HOUSING
Asnières (Haut-de-Seine)
Invited competition
160 condominiums and 50 units of social housing
Client: SMCI Ile-de-France
Project management: JB/ES with Dominique Perrault
Team: Catherine Dormoy, Lionel Loris, Line Sattler
Perspectives: Vincent Lafont
24 000 m²

CULTURAL COMPLEX
Alfortville (Val-de-Marne)
Competition
Theatre hall for 1,500, auditorium for 300, rehearsal and production studios, media library, exhibition space
Client: Ville d'Alfortville
Project management: JB/ES with Jean-Michel Wilmotte

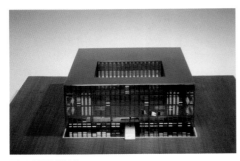

TAX OFFICE Nîmes

E.N.S.M.A. Poitiers

EDUCATIONAL OFFICE Rouen

Team: Catherine Dormoy, Frigo,
Jean-Michel Reynier
Special effects: Richard Peduzi
Building technology: Serete
Perspectives: Louis Paillard
22 000 m²

SPORTS HALL IN PARIS
Rue des Rigoles, Paris 20th arrondisse-
ment
Conversion of a Baltar-type hall to a neigh-
bourhood sports facility
Client: Ville de Paris, Direction de
l'Architecture, SLA 20
Project leader: Isabelle Vasseur
Assistant: Danièle Forte
Building technology: Arcora, Bethac
Value engineering: Ripeau
1 500 m² – completed 1992

1991

UNIVERSITY OF SOCIAL SCIENCES
Strasbourg (Bas-Rhin)
Invited competition
Departments of philosophy, linguistics and
communication, arts and music
Client: Ministère de l'Education Nationale,
de la Jeunesse et des Sports; Académie de
Strasbourg

Team: Catherine Dormoy, David Long,
Danièle Forte
Acoustics: Lasa
Building technology: OTH Est
Perspectives: Vincent Lafont
8 000 m²

TAX OFFICE
Nîmes (Gard)
Design / build competition
Offices, reception areas
Client: Ministère des Finances
Project management: JB/ES with
Nicolas Crégut
Project leader: Jean-Michel Reynier
Building technology: OTCE
Contractor: BEC Construction
Illustrations: Vincent Lafont
Model: Eric Chicaez
6 200 m²

EDUCATIONAL OFFICE OF ROUEN
Rue de Fontenelle, Rouen (Seine-Mari-
time)
Competition
Addition to and renovation of the rector-
ship offices
Client: Ministère de l'Education Nationale,
de la Jeunesse et des Sports
Académie de Rouen
Team: Igor Demidoff, Stanislas Melun

Building technology: Geciba, Bethac
Value engineering: Ripeau
Perspectives: Vincent Lafont
Model: Eric Chicaez
8 600 m²

UNIVERSITY INSTITUTE OF TECH-
NOLOGY
Lieusaint (Seine-et-Marne)
Competition – first prize
Department 2, Industrial Maintenance
Client: Ministère de l'Éducation Nationale
Client's representative: SCARIF
Project leader: Jean-Michel Reynier
Artist: Anna Pricoupenko
Building technology: OTH Bâtiments
3 000 m² – completed 1992

ECOLE NATIONALE SUPÉRIEURE DE
MÉCANIQUE ET D'AÉRONAUTIQUE –
FUTUROSCOPE (E.N.S.M.A.)
Poitiers (Vienne)
Competition
Offices, workshops, classrooms
Client: Ministère de l'Education Nationale,
de la Jeunesse et des Sports; Académie de
Poitiers
Team: Jean-Michel Reynier, David Long
Building technology: Serete
Model: Eric Chicaez
21 000 m²

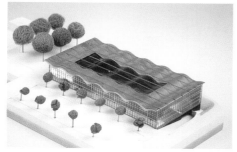
FOREIGN CITIZENS' RECEPTION CENTRE
Bobigny

HIGH SCHOOL Nimes

ECOLE NATIONALE OF MUSIC AND DANCE
Chalon-sur-Saône

ADMINISTRATIVE CENTRE
Saint-Germain-en-Laye

FOREIGN CITIZENS' RECEPTION CENTRE
Bobigny (Seine-Saint-Denis)
Competition
Offices and reception areas
Client: Ministère de l'Intérieur;
Préfecture de Seine-Saint-Denis
Project leader: Vincent Marchand
Assistant: Jean-Michel Reynier
Roofing engineer: Marc Malinowsky
Building technology: OTH Bâtiments
Model: Eric Chicaez
8 500 m²

ADMINISTRATIVE CENTRE
Rue Léon Desoyer, Saint-Germain-en-Laye
(Yvelines)
Competition – first prize
Office and public services, parking
Client: Ville de Saint-Germain-en-Laye
Team competition: Igor Demidoff
Project leaders: Jean-Michel Reynier
(studies), Isabelle Vasseur (site)
Structural engineer for glass: Marc
Malinowsky
Furniture: Eric Pouget
Building technology: OTH Bâtiments
Perspectives: Vincent Lafont
7 000 m² – completed 1994

CENTRAL COMMANDING POST, GARAGE, WORKSHOPS OF VAL DE RENNES
Ligne J.F. Kennedy / La Poterie, Rennes
(Ille-et-Vilaine)
Competition – first prize
Client: SEMTCAR
Project management: JB/ES with "Avant-Travaux"
Building technology: Matra
10 000 m² – completed 1999

1992

NIMES HIGH SCHOOL
Bd Salvador Allende, Nîmes (Gard)
Competition
High school for 2,500 students
Client: Région Languedoc-Roussillon
Project management: JB/ES with
Nicolas Crégut
Project leader: Jean-Michel Reynier
Team: Nathalie Brilman, Alain Debords
Structural engineer: René Vial – Fluides:
Logibat
Value engineering: Algoé
Perspectives: Thierry Lacoste
Model: Eric Chicaez
10 000 m²

IRONWORKS-MODELWORKS
Technocentre Renault, Guyancourt
(Yvelines)
Competition
Development of raw pieces
Client: RENAULT SA
Team: Malcolm Nouvel,
Elsa Cortesse-Vincent
Value engineering: Delta
Model: David Topani
10 000 m²

ECOLE NATIONALE OF MUSIC AND DANCE
Quartier Saint Cosme – Châlon-sur-Saône
(Saône-et-Loire)
Competition – first prize
Auditorium, classrooms, dance studios,
electronic-acoustic studio
Client: Ville de Chalon-sur-Saône
Project leader: George Yiontis
Team: Bach Nguyen, Victor Fuentes
Special effects: Michel Rioualec
Acoustics: Lasa
Furniture: Valérie Faugeras
Landscaping: Méristème
Facade consultant: Jean-Louis Besnard
Structural engineer: Terrell Rooke
Flows: Bethac
Value engineering: Delta
Graphics: Bernard Baissait and Cie
6 000 m² – completed 1995

TECHNOCENTRE LABORATORIES Guyancourt

EXHIBITION Pavillon de l'Arsenal, Paris

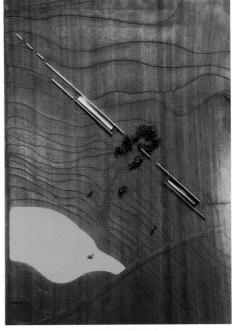
LOUIS DERBRE FOUNDATION Ernée

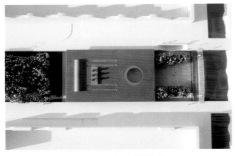
TECHNOCENTRE RESTAURANT Guyancourt

HIGH SCHOOL Rozay-en-Brie

FRANCE TELECOM – OCTAL
Montpellier (Hérault)
Offices
Client: France Telecom
Project management: JB/ES with Nicolas
Crégut
Team: George Yiontis, Bach Nguyen
Structural engineer: René Vial – Flows:
Logibat
Value engineering: Algoé
Perspectives: Vincent Lafont
Model: David Topani
3 500 m²

TECHNOCENTRE LABORATORIES
Guyancourt (Yvelines)
Competition – first prize
Laboratories, industrial hall, offices
Client: Renault SA
Team (competition): George Yiontis
Project leaders: Igor Demidoff, then Vin-
cent Marchand, Jean-Michel Reynier
Team: Lionel Renouf, Geneviève Shater
Model: David Topani
30 000 m² – completed 1998

TECHNOCENTRE RESTAURANT
Guyancourt (Yvelines)
Competition
Client: Renault SA
Team (competition): Jean-Michel Reynier
Kitchen consultant: SA Huron

Flows: Inex
Value engineering: DELTA
Model: Jean-Michel Françoise
3 000 m²

EXHIBITION "100 YEARS OF HOUSING"
Pavillon de l'Arsenal, Paris 4th arron-
dissement
"Water and gas on every floor"
Special effects, exhibition signage
Client: Ville de Paris
Assistant: Philippe Vasseur
Exhibition representative: Jacques Lucan
800 m² – Exhibition dates: September
1992 – January 1993

LA TOUR DES DAMES HIGH SCHOOL
Rozay-en-Brie (Seine-et-Marne)
Design build competition – first prize
Client: Région Ile-de-France
Client's representative: DDE de Seine-et-
Marne
Project leader: Vincent Marchand
Team: Malcolm Nouvel (competition),
Pawel Kornecki (studies and site)
Artist: François Seigneur
Building technology: OTH Bâtiments
Contractor: Dezelus Construction
Chambon
Perspectives: Vincent Lafont
First phase: 6 500 m² – completed 1993

LOUIS DERBRE FOUNDATION
Ernée (Mayenne)
Client: Conseil Général de la Mayenne –
Ville d'Ernée
Workshop, foundry, exhibition space for
sculptor Louis Derbré
Assistant: Isabelle Vasseur
Model: Eric Chicaez
1 000 m² – completed 1993

1993

UNIVERSITY INSTITUTE OF TECHNOLO-
GY OF LIEUSAINT (Departments 3 and 4)
Melun-Sénart (Seine-et-Marne)
Competition – first prize
Client: Ministère de l'Éducation Nationale
Client's representative: SCARIF
Project leader: Jean-Michel Reynier
Assistant: Vincent Mégrot
Building technology: OTH Bâtiments
7 500 m² – completed 1993

CACHAREL HEADQUARTERS
Le Colisée – Nîmes (Gard)
Redesign of the Offices and show room in
the building by Kisho Kurokawa
Client: Société Cacharel
Project leader: Christophe Kuntz
Assistant: Valérie Faugeras (furniture)

CACHAREL HEADQUARTERS Nîmes

BANQUE DE FRANCE Montpellier

FRENCH CULTURAL CENTRE Port-Louis

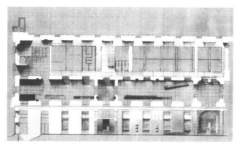

LOUVRE SCHOOL Paris

LE SOU MEDICAL HEADQUARTERS Paris

Scenic lighting, sound, signage: LM Communiquer
Sculptor: Gatimalau
Building technology: Acora
Perspectives: Vincent Lafont
5 000 m² – completed 1994

BANQUE DE FRANCE REGIONAL HEADQUARTERS
Avenue de Lodève, Montpellier (Hérault)
Competition – first prize
Banque de France regional headquarters
Client: Banque de France, Direction de l'Immobilier
Project leaders: Christophe Kuntz, George Yiontis, Bach Nguyen
Assistant: Jacques Lévy-Bencheton
Facade consultant: Jean-Louis Besnard
Concrete consultant: Jean-Pierre Aury
Furniture: Valérie Faugeras
Building technology: Serete Constructions
Perspectives: Anne and Denis Cleary
Sculptor: Gatimalau
6 500 m² – completed 1996

LOUVRE SCHOOL
Aile de Flore – Grand Louvre, Paris 1st arrondissement
Competition
Auditorium, offices, classrooms and library on the ground floor and basement levels of the Louvre

Client: Etablissement Public du Grand Louvre
Assistant: Philippe Vasseur
Building technology: OTH Bâtiment
Perspectives: Vincent Lafont
4 200 m²

CENTRAL LAW COURTS
Grasse (Alpes-Maritimes)
Competition
Tribunal de Grande Instance, Tribunal d'Instance, Tribunal de Commerce, Conseil de Prud'hommes
Client: Ministère de la Justice
Operations management: DDE des Alpes-Maritimes
Team: Myriam Dao, Jean-Michel Reynier
Structural engineer: YRM – Flows: Inex
Value engineering: Delta
Perspectives: Didier Ghislain, Vincent Lafont
20 000 m²

FRENCH CULTURAL CENTRE
Port-Louis (Mauritius, Indian Ocean)
Competition
Exhibition space, restaurant, workshops, conference hall, theatre hall
Client: Ministère de la Coopération
Project Management: JB/ES with Lampotang and Siew

Assistant: George Yiontis
Structural engineer: OTH International
Perspectives: Vincent Lafont
2 600 m²

EDUCATIONAL CENTRE OF DIJON
University Campus, Dijon (Côte-d'Or)
Competition
Offices and public services
Client: Ministère de l'Education Nationale – Académie de Dijon
Assistant: Igor Demidoff
Landscaping: Kathryn Gustafson
Structural engineer: YRM – Flows: Inex / Ingespie
Value engineering: Delta
12 000 m²

LE SOU MEDICAL HEADQUARTERS
Rue de Bellefond – Paris 9th arrondissement
Conversion of a former warehouse to office use
Client: Compagnie d'assurances "le Sou Médical"
Project leader: Vincent Marchand
Assistant: Pawel Kornecki
Structural engineer: Geciba – Flows: Bethac
Value engineering: Philippe Talbot
1 000 m² – completed 1994

FIRST AID CENTRE Le Blanc-Mesnil

FRENCH CHAMBER OF COMMERCE AND
INDUSTRY Paris

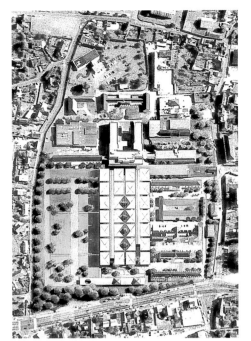

UNIVERSITY HOSPITAL CENTRE Caen

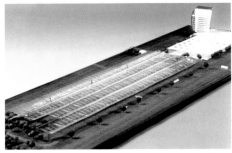

GLASBAU SEELE Factory and offices Gersthofen

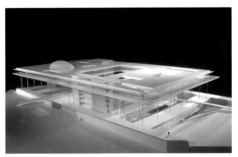

FEDERAL CHANCELERY Berlin

UNIVERSITY OF MEDICINE
Tours (Indre-et-Loire)
Client: Rectorat de Tours
Team: Vincent Marchand, Igor Demidoff,
Vincent Mégrot
Building technology: IMC
4 500 m²

1994

FIRST AID CENTRE
Le Blanc-Mesnil (Seine-Saint-Denis)
Competition – first prize
Client: Préfecture de Police
Project leader: Jean-Michel Reynier
Structural engineer: Geciba – Flows:
Bethac
Value engineering: Delta
Perspectives: Vincent Lafont
Model: David Topani
5 000 m² – completed 1998

SEAT OF THE ORGANISATION OF
FRENCH CHAMBERS OF COMMERCE
AND INDUSTRY
Boulevard Saint-Jacques, Paris 14th arron-
dissement
Competition
Offices, conference centre, restaurants
Client: SCI Saint-Jacques ACFCI
Client's representative: SCIC-AMO

Aménageur: S.A.D.M.
Project leaders: Jean-Michel Reynier, Igor
Demidoff
Building technology: Sfica
Perspectives: François Robain
Model: Jean-Michel Françoise
8 500 m²

UNIVERSITY HOSPITAL CENTRE
Caen (Calvados)
Competition – first prize
Client: Centre Hospitalier Universitaire
Project leaders: Toshio Sekiguchi (compe-
tition), Jean-Michel Reynier (studies)
Team: Vincent Mégrot, Federico Masotto,
Pierre-Emmanuel Droste, Victor Fuentes,
Adélaïde Borniche
Building technology: Serete Constructions
Perspectives: Vincent Lafont
14 000 m² – First phase completed 1997

GLASBAU SEELE
Factory and offices
Gersthofen (Germany)
Invited competition
Client: Glasbau Seele
Project leader: Matthias Bauer
Architect engineer: Vincent Marchand
Team: Jean-Michel Reynier, Igor Demidoff,
Jacques Lévy-Bencheton, Michel Plaxine
Structural engineer: Alto (Marc
Malinowsky)

Flows: Kuehn Bauer + Partner (Munich)
Lighting: Christian Bartenbach (Munich)
Acoustics: Lasa
Perspectives: Anne and Denis Cleary
30 000 m²

FEDERAL CHANCELERY
Berlin (Germany)
Invited competition
Client: Federal Republic of Germany
Team: Igor Demidoff, Jean-Michel Reynier,
George Yiontis, Matthias Bauer, Pierre-
Emmanuel Droste, Vincent Mégrot, Victor
Fuentes
Landscaping: Philippe Niez, Alexandra
Schmidt
Structural engineer: RFR
Facades: ARCORA
Video images: Pierre Miquel – Environ
Perspectives: Vincent Lafont
110 000 m²

HENRI SELLIER HIGH SCHOOL
Livry-Gargan (Seine-Saint-Denis)
Design build competition
Client: Région Ile-de-France
Project leader: Vincent Marchand
Building technology: Technip Seri Con-
struction
Contractor: Dezellus Construct. Chambon
Perspectives: Vincent Lafont
8 000 m²

RESIDENTIAL BUILDING Paris

MUSEUM Saint-Pierre et Miquelon

FRENCH EMBASSY (2nd) Kampala (Uganda)

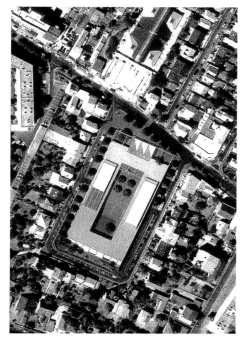

GUSTAVE EIFFEL HIGH SCHOOL
Rueil-Malmaison

RESIDENTIAL BUILDING RUE NEUVE TOLBIAC
Rue Neuve Tolbiac, Paris 13th arrondissement
Competition – first prize
95 units of social housing
Client: La Sablière
Project leaders: Vincent Marchand (competition), Jean-Michel Reynier (studies), Isabelle Vasseur (site)
Team: Isabelle Vasseur, Bach Nguyen, George Yiontis, Federico Masotto, Valérie Faugeras
Artist: Anna Pricoupenko
Structural engineer: Geciba – Flows: Bethac
Value engineering: Delta
Perspectives: Vincent Lafont
Model: David Topani
10 000 m² – Completed 1997

VEHICLE TESTING CENTRE
Guyancourt (Yvelines)
Competition
Client: Renault SA
Team: Igor Demidoff, George Yiontis, Lionel Renouf
Building technology: Sogelerg
Value engineering: Delta
Model: David Topani
Surface: 12 500 m²

1995

MUSEUM OF SAINT-PIERRE ET MIQUELON
Saint-Pierre (French oversea territory)
Competition
Museum and archive complex
Client: Ministère de la Coopération Conseil Général de Saint-Pierre et Miquelon
Client's representative: SODEPAR
Client's team: SCET DOM-TOM
Assistant: Igor Demidoff
Museography: Jean-François Bodin
Building technology: OTH International
Perspectives: Vincent Lafont
2 500 m²

GUSTAVE EIFFEL HIGH SCHOOL
Rueil-Malmaison (Hauts-de-Seine)
Competition
Client: Conseil Régional d'Ile-de-France SEM 92
Project leader: Vincent Marchand
Team: Jean-Michel Reynier, Vincent Mégrot, Jacques Lévy-Bencheton
Building technology: Technip Seri Construction
Perspectives: Vincent Lafont
Model: David Topani
12 000 m²

FRENCH EMBASSY (2nd)
Kampala (Uganda)
Competition
Client: Ministère des Affaires Étrangères
Building technology: Sincoba
Perspectives: Jacques Aillaud
2 000 m²

TERRAGE-BOUTRON HOUSING
Paris 10th arrondissement
Competition
Client: Office Public d'Aménagement et de Construction de Paris
Project leader: Jean-Michel Reynier
Value engineering: Philippe Talbot
Perspectives: Vincent Lafont
2 400 m²

RESIDENTIAL BUILDINGS PARIS
Rue de Flandre – Paris 19th arrondissement
Competition – first prize
Client: Office Public d'Aménagement et de Construction de Paris
Project leader: Isabelle Vasseur
Assistant: Jean-Michel Reynier
Building technology: OTH Habitation
Perspectives: Didier Ghislain
5 200 m² – completed 1999

RESIDENTIAL BUILDINGS Paris

SAINT-PIERRE INSTITUTE Palavas-les-Flots

VALEO
Limoges (Haute-Vienne)
Proposal for the modernisation of
the Valéo site
Client: Valéo (friction materials)
Project leader: Vincent Marchand
Structural engineer: Terrell Rooke
Flows: Bethac
Value engineering: Philippe Talbot
Associés
4 000 m²

COLLEGE ANDRE MALRAUX
Asnières (Hauts-de-Seine)
Competition
Client: Conseil Général des Hauts-de-Seine
Team: Vincent Marchand, Vincent Mégrot
7 600 m²

SAINT-PIERRE INSTITUTE
Palavas-les-Flots (Hérault)
Invited competition – first prize
Children's hospital, remedial therapy
Client: Oeuvre Montpelliéraine des
Enfants à la Mer (O.M.E.M.)
Client's representative: SCIC Développe-
ment
Project leader: Jean-Michel Reynier
(studies), Christophe Kuntz (site)
Team: Jacques Lévy-Bencheton, Federico
Masotto, Alberto Medem
Signage: Sabine Rosant S.R.P.C.

Landscaping: Christine and Michel Péna
Building technology: Jacobs-Serete
Perspectives: Jacques Aillaud
13 000 m² – completed 1999

CACHAREL PARIS
Rue Etienne Marcel, Paris 1st arrondisse-
ment
Show room for collections
Client: Sté Cacharel
Project leader: Christophe Kuntz
Assistant: Valérie Faugeras
300 m² – completed 1995

FRANCE ELECTRICITY (EDF) OFFICES
Quai Dedion Bouton, Puteaux (Hauts-
de-Seine)
Competition
EDF Agency – Offices
Client: EDF
Project leader: Igor Demidoff
Building technology: Betom
11 000 m²

1996

PROSPER CHUBERT HOSPITAL CENTRE
Vannes (Morbihan)
Competition
Renovation and addition to the hospital
centre

Client: Centre Hospitalier Prosper Chubert
Project leader: Vincent Marchand
Team: Eduardo Arroyo, Alberto Medem
Landscaping: Christine and Michel Péna
Building technology: Sogelerg
Perspectives: Jacques Aillaud, Vincent
Lafont
40 000 m²

LA PAILLADE MAINTENANCE CENTRE
Montpellier (Hérault)
First tram line in the Montpellier suburbs
Competition, Garage Workshops
Client: SMTUM
Assistant: Igor Demidoff
Landscaping: Christine and Michel Péna
Building technology: GEC Ingénierie
Perspectives: Jacques Aillaud
8 600 m²

CHATEAU D'HENNEMONT
International High School of Saint-Ger-
main-en-Laye (Yvelines)
Renovation and reorganisation of a 19th
century castle: lecture hall, reception halls,
housing
Client: Ministère de l'Éducation Nationale
Client's representative: DDE des Yvelines
Project leaders: Philippe Vasseur (studies),
Isabelle Vasseur (site)
Structural engineer: Geciba – Flows:
Bethac

CHATEAU D'HENNEMONT
Saint-Germain-en-Laye

UNIVERSITY HOSPITAL CENTRE Reims

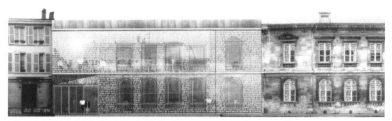

MUNICIPAL LIBRARY FOR REGIONAL AFFAIRS Châlons-en-Champagne

Value engineering: AEI
6 000 m² – completed January 2000

FISCAL AUTHORITY RHONE
Lyon (Rhône)
Competition
Reorganisation of the computer centre of
the Departmental Fiscal Authority
Client: Ministère de l'Économie, des Fi-
nances et de la Privatisation
Project leader: Vincent Marchand
Building technology: Bethac
Value engineering: Philippe Talbot
5 000 m²

1997

LYCEE FRANÇAIS
Frankfurt (Germany)
Competition
Client: Ministère des Affaires Etrangères
Team: Wolfgang Dievernich, Jean-Michel
Reynier, Jacques Lévy-Bencheton, Vincent
Mégrot
Building technology: Sogelerg, Lahmeyer
international GmbH
Perspectives: Jérôme Sigwalt
8 000 m²

HIGH ENVIRONMENTAL STANDARDS
(H.Q.E.) BUILDING PROGRAM HIGH
SCHOOL
Caudry (Nord)
Design build competition
Client: Conseil Général du Nord-Pas-de-
Calais
Project management: JB/ES with Graph
Architectes
Project leader: Vincent Marchand
Landscaping: Landscaping Bocage
Environmental building technology: Alter
Ego conseil
Coordinator for environmental issues:
Pierre Diaz-Pedregal
Contractor: Rabot-Duthilleul
Perspectives: Karine Herman and Jérôme
Sigwalt / Philippe Harden
12 000 m²

MUNICIPAL LIBRARY FOR REGIONAL
AFFAIRS
Châlons-en-Champagne (Marne)
Competition
Client: Ville de Châlons-en-Champagne
Team: Jean-Michel Reynier,
Jacques Lévy-Bencheton, Vincent Mégrot
Building technology: Technip Seri Con-
struction
Perspectives: Vincent Lafont, Philippe
Harden
6 800 m²

UNIVERSITY HOSPITAL CENTRE
Reims (Marne)
Competition
IGGOMEP – Institute of genetics,
gynaecologie-obstetrics and perinatal
medecine
Client: Centre Hospitalier Universitaire
Team: Vincent Marchand, Gérold
Zimmerli, Jean-Michel Reynier
Building technology: Serete Constructions
Perspectives: Philippe Harden
Model: David Topani
11 000 m²

CARPENTRY
Annecy (Haute-Savoie)
Workshop and show room
Client: Techniques d'Agencement
Project leader: Christophe Kuntz
Building technology: Bethac
Perspectives: Philippe Harden
1 600 m² – completed 1998

PREFABRICATED BUILDINGS
Jussieu Campus, Paris 5th arrondissement
Design build competition – first prize
Temporary buildings erected for the
duration of the asbestos removal in the
university
Client: Université Paris 6 Pierre et Marie
Curie
Client's consultant: G3A

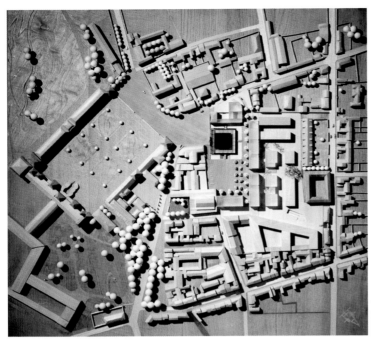

QUARTIER BOUFFLERS – HOTEL DE FERRARE Fontainebleau

SCHOOL OF ARCHITECTURE Montpellier

BAUER STADIUM Saint-Ouen

Contractor: Léon Grosse
Perspectives: Vincent Lafont
Model: Bruno Isambert
7 000 m² – completed 1998

FORMULA 1 FACTORY – PROST GRAND
PRIX
Versailles (Yvelines)
Design build competition
Workshops laboratories and offices for the
research and development of high tech
automobile prototypes
Client: Ville de Versailles
Client's team: AFTRP
Assistant: Jean-Michel Reynier
Contractor: Léon Grosse
Perspectives: Philippe Harden
7 000 m² – unrealised

1998

QUARTIER BOUFFLERS – HOTEL DE
FERRARE
Fontainebleau (Seine-et-Marne)
Architect developer competition
New quarter facing the palace: housing,
shops, business, offices, underground
parking and public facilities
Client: Ville de Fontainebleau
Client's team: AFTRP
Developer: SEDAF

Project management: JB/ES with F. Jestaz
and E. Legleye
Team: Jean-Michel Reynier, Jacques Lévy-
Bencheton
Landscaping: Bruel / Delmar
Programme: Dourdin Consultant
Perspectives: Vincent Lafont
20 000 m²

SCHOOL OF ARCHITECTURE
Montpellier (Hérault)
Addition to the school of architecture of
Languedoc-Roussillon
Client: Ministère de la Culture
Team: Karine Herman, Jérôme Sigwalt
Building technology: Beterem
Value engineering: Philippe Talbot
2 800 m²

BAUER STADIUM
Saint-Ouen (Seine-Saint-Denis)
Design build competition
New stadium for "Red Star" at the heart of
the redevelopment of disused Wonder and
Valéo industrial sites
Client: Ville de Saint-Ouen
Project management: JB/ES with Pierre
Rigaudeau
Team: G. Bilcandou, Adélaïde Borniche,
K. Jensen, Jacques Lévy-Bencheton,
Vincent Mégrot, Jean-Michel Reynier,
N. Soumagnac

Contractor: Léon Grosse
Perspectives: Vincent Lafont
Model: Rod Marawi
25 000 m²

UNIVERSITY HOSPITAL CENTRE
Tours (Indre-et-Loire)
Competition
Addition to Trousseau hospital
Client: CHU de Tours
Project management: JB/ES with Roger
Ivars and Jean Christophe Ballet
Team: Vincent Marchand, Gérold Zimmerli
Building technology: Serete Constructions
Perspectives: Vincent Lafont
Model: L. Salomé
14 000 m²

ECOLE NATIONALE OF MUSIC, DANCE
AND THEATRE
Le Havre (Seine-Maritime)
Competition – first prize
Auditorium, classrooms, electronic-acou-
stics studios
Client: Ville du Havre
Project leaders: Jean-Michel Reynier (com-
petition), Jean-François Bourdet (studies),
Isabelle Vasseur (site)
Structural engineer: Terrell International –
Flows: Bethac
Special effects: Changement à Vue
Acoustics: Delphi

UNIVERSITY HOSPITAL CENTRE Tours

UNIVERSITY HOSPITAL CENTRE Caen

UNIVERSITY HOSPITAL CENTRE Tours

BOURGET CLINIC Le Bourget

PAUL VALERY UNIVERSITY Montpellier

Value engineering: Philippe Talbot
Perspectives: Philippe Harden
8 600 m² – 1st phase completed 2002

BOURGET CLINIC
Le Bourget (Seine-Saint-Denis)
Invited competition
Clinic with 300 beds
Client: Générale de Santé
Project management: JB/ES with Gérold
Zimmerli
Team: Malcolm Nouvel, Jean-Michel
Reynier, Vincent Mégrot, Jacques Lévy-
Bencheton, Philippe Harden
Perspectives: Didier Ghislain
25 000 m²

PAUL VALERY UNIVERSITY
Montpellier (Hérault)
Competition – first prize
Building for theatre instruction including
theatre, lecture hall, classrooms
Client: Ministère de l'Education Nationale
– Rectorat de Montpellier
Operation management: DDE de l'Hérault
Team: Jean-Michel Reynier, Vincent
Mégrot, Christophe Kuntz (studies),
Nicolas Crégut (site)
Building technology: Beterem
Value engineering: Philippe Talbot
Perspectives: Vincent Lafont
5 200 m² – completed 2002

CONTE FACTORY
Boulogne-sur-Mer (Pas-de-Calais)
Invited competition – first prize
Factory for manufacture, production and
storage
Client: CONTE
Project management: JB/ES with J. Jestaz
Perspectives: Philippe Harden
25 000 m² – unrealised

UNIVERSITY HOSPITAL CENTRE
Tours (Indre-et-Loire)
Competition – first prize
Renovation of Clocheville hospital
Reorganisation – addition of the
pediatric hospital, technical level,
beds and pharmacy
Client: CHU de Tours
Project management: JB/ES with Roger
Ivars and Jean-Christophe Ballet
Project leader: Vincent Marchand
Assistant: Jean-Michel Reynier (compe-
tition)
Studies: Tahar Cheref
Building technology: Sogelerg
Perspectives: Vincent Lafont
Model: L. Salomé
10 000 m² – completed 2003

UNIVERSITY HOSPITAL CENTRE
Caen (Calvados)
Renovation – addition to the central
pharmacy of Clémenceau hospital
Client: Centre Hospitalier Universitaire
Assistant: Alberto Medem
Building technology: Serete Construction
3 500 m² – completed 1998

RESOURCE CENTRE FOR MULTIMEDIA
DOCUMENTATION
Ilot Ségur-Fontenoy – Ministère de
l'Emploi et de la Solidarité, Paris 7th
arrondissement
Competition – first prize
Library, lecture and consultation hall
Client: Ministère de l'Emploi et de la
Solidarité
Team: Jean-Michel Reynier (competition),
Christophe Kuntz (studies), Camille
Nourrit (furniture), Philippe Vasseur (site)
Building technology: Sfica
Value engineering: AEI
3 000 m² – completed 2001

UNIVERSITY OF PARIS IX – DAUPHINE
Place du Maréchal de Lattre de Tassigny,
Paris 16th arrondissement
Competition – first prize
Redesign of the main lecture hall
Client: Ministère de l'Education Nationale,
Université Paris IX

UNIVERSITY OF PARIS IX – DAUPHINE Paris

MARCEL DEPREZ HIGH SCHOOL Paris

LYON-SUD MEDICAL PAVILION Lyon

HOSPITAL CENTRE Rambouillet

Client's representative: G3A
Building technology: Technip
Assistant: Philippe Vasseur
1 500 m² – completed 2001

1999

MARCEL DEPREZ HIGH SCHOOL
Rue de la Roquette, Paris 11th arrondissement
Competition
Client: Conseil Régional d'Ile de France
Client's representative: G3A
Team: Jean-Michel Reynier, Vincent Mégrot, Jacques Lévy-Bencheton, Lionel Renouf, Camille Nourrit
Building technology: Sogelerg
Perspectives: Vincent Lafont
7 000 m²

MINISTRY OF LABOUR AND SOCIAL AFFAIRS
Ilot Ségur-Fontenoy, Paris 7th arrondissement
Competition
Redesign of the circulation on Fontenoy-Ségur island
Client: Ministère de l'Emploi et de la Solidarité
Team: Jean-Michel Reynier, Camille Nourrit
Building technology: Sfica

Value engineering: AEI
Perspectives: Vincent Lafont
3 000 m²

LYON-SUD MEDICAL PAVILION
Lyon (Rhône)
Competition
Creation of three hubs: cardiology, endocrinology and pneumology
Client: Hospices Civils de Lyon
Project management: JB/ES with Jean-Paul Rouillat
Project leader: Vincent Marchand
Assistant: Stéphanie Boisson
Structural engineer: EEG – Flows: SIRR
Value engineering: Voutay
Perspectives: Christophe Valtin-Umlaut
26 000 m²

HOSPITAL CENTRE
Dreux (Eure-et-Loire)
Competition
Remedial therapy services
Client: Centre Hospitalier de Dreux
Team: Karine Herman, Jérôme Sigwalt
Building technology: Setae
6 000 m²

TOWN HALL PARKING
Châlon-sur-Saône (Saône-et-Loire)
Invited competition – first prize
Underground parking for 480 cars

Client: Parcofrance
Assistant: Philippe Vasseur
Project leader realisation: Lionel Renouf
Perspectives: Philippe Harden
12 000 m² – completed 2001

MULTIPLEX
Châlon-sur-Saône (Saône-et-Loire)
Developer architect consultancy
9 movie theatres of 400, 250 and 150 seats, shops, restaurant, housing, parking
Developer: Dumez-Rhône Alpes / GTM / ADIRA (cinema)
Assistant: Jacques Lévy-Bencheton
Consultant: Claude Fusée
Perspectives: Philippe Harden
15 000 m²

HOSPITAL CENTRE
Dreux (Eure-et-Loire)
Competition
Remedial therapy services
Client: Centre Hospitalier de Dreux
Team: Karine Herman, Jérôme Sigwalt
Building technology: Setae
6 000 m²

HOSPITAL CENTRE
Rambouillet (Yvelines)
Competition
Reorganisation of the technical platform and the M.C.O.-beds

TOWN HALL PARKING Chalon-sur-Saône

MULTIPLEX Chalon-sur-Saône

OFFICES Avenue de Saint-Cloud, Versailles

ENVIRONMENTAL AND ENERGIE SAVINGS
AGENCY (ADEME) Angers

MAISON BLANCHE PSYCHIATRIC HOSPITAL
Paris

Client: Centre Hospitalier de Rambouillet
Project leader: Vincent Marchand
Hospital consultant: Gérold Zimmerli
Building technology: Sogelerg
Perpectives: Vincent Lafont
11 500 m²

JUSSIEU UNIVERSITY – ESCLANGON
BUILDING
Rue de Jussieu, Paris 6th arrondissement
Design build competition
Industrialised building for the temporary
accomodation of teaching and research
Client: EPA Jussieu
Client's representative: G3A
Contractor: Léon Grosse
Project leader: Jean-Michel Reynier
Team: Vincent Mégrot, Jacques Lévy-
Bencheton, Lionel Renouf
Perspectives: Christophe Valtin-Umlaut
9 000 m²

ENVIRONMENTAL AND ENERGIE
SAVINGS AGENCY (ADEME)
Angers (Maine-et-Loire)
Competition – first prize
Social seat, test building and prototype of
the high environmental standards ap-
proach and durable development. Offices,
conference centre, restaurant
Client: Agence de l'Environnement et de la
Maîtrise de l'Énergie

Client's representative: SARA
Programers: CPO Programmation –
Nuance Ergonomie – Tribu
Project management: JB/ES with
Jean-Pierre Bastide
Project leader: Jean-Michel Reynier
Team: Isabelle Vasseur, Vincent Mégrot,
Marie-HélèneTorcq
Landscaping: Bruel Delmar
Coordinator for environmental issues:
Pierre Diaz-Pedregal
Building technology: Séchaud and Bossuyt
Perspectives: Vincent Lafont
10 000 m² – completed 2002

OFFICES
Avenue de Saint-Cloud, Versailles
(Yvelines)
Client: Léon Grosse
Assistant: Isabelle Vasseur
Perspectives: Vincent Lafont
4 000 m² – completed 2002

MAISON BLANCHE PSYCHIATRIC
HOSPITAL
Rue d'Hauteville, Paris 10th arrondisse-
ment
Competition
Saint Martin section (60 beds) and La
Tour d'Auvergne (40 beds)
Client: Etablissement Publique de Santé de
Maison Blanche

Client's representative: SCIC Développe-
ment
Project leader: Jean-Michel Reynier
Assistant: Vincent Mégrot
Building technology: Setae
Value engineering: Philippe Talbot
6 000 m²

NATIONAL CENTRE FOR THE
ORGANISATION OF AGRICULTURAL
STRUCTURES (CNASEA)
Limoges (Haute-Vienne)
Competition
Relocation to Limoges of the social seat
of CNASEA: offices and computer centres.
Client: Ministère de l'Agriculture/CNASEA
Client's representative: G3A
Project leader: Jean-François Bourdet
Team: Astrid Rappel, Alexis Lorch,
K. Berger
Building technology: Séchaud and Bossuyt
Perspectives: Eric Anton
Model: Alpha Volumes
10 000 m²

OFFICES
Hérouville Saint-Clair (Calvados)
Space planning: Shema
Client: SOGEA
Project leader: Jean-Michel Reynier
Assistant: Jean-François Bourdet
3 000 m²

NATIONAL CENTRE FOR AGRICULTURAL
STRUCTURES Limoges

NATEXIS BANQUES POPULAIRES Charenton

JUSSIEU UNIVERSITY Paris

HOSPITAL CENTRE OF HAUT-ANJOU
Château-Gontier

ILOT VILLOT-RAPEE HOUSING Paris

GLASS MUSEUM
Sars-Poteries (Nord)
Workshops, exhibition spaces
Project leader: Jean-Michel Reynier
Perspectives: Philippe Harden
800 m²

2000

NATEXIS BANQUES POPULAIRES
Charenton-le-Pont (Val-de-Marne)
Invited competition
Administrative seat, conference centre,
restaurant
Client: Natexis Banques Populaires
Project leaders: Jean-Michel Reynier,
Vincent Marchand
Team: Jacques Levy-Bencheton,
Jean-François Bourdet
Building technology: Philippe Talbot /
Béthac
Security consultant: Casso / Seet Secoba
Perspectives: Eric Anton / Vincent Lafont /
Laurent Hochberg
Model: Alpha Volumes / Rod Marawi
53 000 m²

L'OREAL CONFERENCE CENTRE
Aulnay-Chanteloup (Seine-Saint-Denis)
Conference centre, restaurant-club, gene-
ral reorganisation of the site

Client: L'OREAL
Flows: Bethac
Value engineering: Philippe Talbot
Perspectives: Laurent Hochberg
Model: Alpha Volumes
5 700 m²

"LES MASSUES" MEDICAL-SURGICAL
CENTRE
Lyon (Rhône)
Invited competition
Addition-renovation of the medical-
surgical reintegration centre
Client: Groupama Assurances
Project management: JB/ES with
Jean-Paul Rouillat
Building technology: Sodeteg
Perspectives: Martignac
14 000 m²

TEXTILE CENTRE
Lyon (Rhône)
Competition
Creation / promotion / communication
centre of the textile and clothing hub of
the Rhône-Alpes Region
Client: UNITEX
Client's representative: SERC
Project management: JB/ES with
Jean-Paul Rouillat
Assistant: Jean-Michel Reynier
Building technology: Matté s.a.

Value engineering: Cabinet Denizou
Perspectives: Laurent Hochberg
3 800 m²

ILOT VILLOT-RAPEE HOUSING
Quai de la Rapée, Paris 12th arrondisse-
ment
Competition
70 units of social housing
Client: OPAC de Paris
Assistant: Jean-Michel Reynier
Perspectives: Didier Ghislain
5 000 m²

HOSPITAL CENTRE OF HAUT-ANJOU
Château-Gontier (Mayenne)
Competition
Technical platform and 150 beds
Client: Centre Hospitalier
Client's representative: DDE
Project management: JB/ES with William
Gohier
Team: Vincent Marchand, Vincent Mégrot,
Christophe Kuntz, Jacques Lévy-Bencheton
Architect hospital consultant: Gérold
Zimmerli
Landscaping: Alfred Peter
Structural engineer and value engineering:
AUA structure – Flows: SETAE
Perspectives: Didier Ghislain
Model: Alpha Volumes
20 000 m²

HOSPITAL CENTRE Cannes

FACULTE D'ASSAS Paris

FRENCH EMBASSY Warsaw (Poland)

HOSPITAL CENTRE Saint-Germain-en-Laye

AWON OFFICES Massy

HOSPITAL CENTRE
Limoges (Indre-et-Loire)
Competition
Mother-child centre
Client: Centre Hospitalier de Limoges
Project leaders: Vincent Marchand,
Jean-Michel Reynier, Tahar Cheref
Building technology: Terrell International –
Flows: Bethac
Value engineering: Philippe Talbot
Perspectives: Vincent Lafont / Laurent
Hochberg
20 500 m²

HOSPITAL CENTRE
Saint-Germain-en-Laye (Yvelines)
Competition
Mother-child centre, rehabilitation
Client: Centre Hospitalier Intercommunal
de Poissy / Saint-Germain-en-Laye
Client's representative: SCIC Développe-
ment
Team: Hélène Planex, Vincent Mégrot
Building technology: SETAE
Perspectives: Philippe Harden
9 200 m²

HOSPITAL CENTRE
Cannes (Alpes-Maritimes)
Competition – first prize
Client: Centre Hospitalier de Cannes

Client's representative: SCIC Développe-
ment
Project management: JB/ES with Architec-
tes Studio Associés (Gilles Gauvain)
Hospital consultant: Gérold Zimmerli
Building technology: Terrell Rooke Asso-
ciés – Utilities supplies: SIRR
Value engineering: Philippe Talbot
Perspectives: Vincent Lafont
Model: Alpha Volumes
55 000 m² – completed 2006

FACULTE D'ASSAS
Rue d'Assas, Paris 6th arrondissement
Competition
Client: Ministère de l'Éducation Nationale
Client's representative: SCAP
Structural engineer: Terrell Rooke Associés
– Flows: Béthode
Value engineering: G.V. Ingénierie
OPC: Gémo
Perspectives: Vincent Lafont

BIOLOGY CENTRE
Lille (Nord)
Competition
Laboratories and offices
Client: CHU de Lille
Team: Jean-François Bourdet, Vincent
Mégrot
Building technology: SETAE

Value engineering: Philippe Duval
Perspectives: Vincent Lafont
Model: Alpha Volumes
18 000 m²

FRENCH EMBASSY
Warsaw (Poland)
Competition – jury's award
Client: Ministère des Affaires Étrangères
Team: Jean-Michel Reynier, Astrid Rappel,
Jacques Lévy-Bencheton, Lionel Renouf
Building technology: Séchaud & Bossuyt /
Bief
Programme: Dourdin consultant
Perspectives: Eric Anton
Model: Alpha Volumes
6 000 m²

AWON OFFICES
Massy (Essonne)
Invited competition – first prize
Client: Awon Group
Team / Client: M.A.P.S.
Structural engineer: Terrell Rooke Associés
– Flows: Béthode
Value engineering: Philippe Talbot
12 000 m²

Assistants

Marie AKAR, Marine ALEXANDRE, Frédéric ALLI-GORIDES, Christèle ANDRIEUX, Eduardo ARRO-YO, Marianne ARTARIT, Éric BABIN, Catherine BAI-BRUNET, Laurent BANDINI, Christian BASSET, Christophe BAUBIL, Matthias BAUER, Élisabeth BEAULIEU, Martin Gonzalo BENAVIDES, K. BER-GER, Véronique BEYRON, Hervé BLETON, Gilles BOCION, Stéphanie BOISSON, Adélaïde BOR-NICHE, Jean-François BOURDET, Laurent BOU-THONNEAU, Gilles BRESARD, Colette BRICE, Nathalie BRILMAN, Claire BRUNET, Véronique BRUNET, Aline CABOURET, Sandrine CARDON, Marc CHASSIN, Guillemette CHENIEUX, Tahar CHEREF, Nicolas CHEVRON, Jean-Christophe CHOTTIN, Thomas CORBASSON, Elsa CORTES-SE-VINCENT, Éric CUGNART, Myriam DAO, So-phie de RENZY-MARTIN, Alain DEBORD, Emma-nuelle DELABY, Gabriel DELAGE, Igor DEMIDOFF, Brune DESALLAIS, Sylvestre DIDIER, Wolfgang DIEVERNICH, Ingrid DOM, Cécile DOMAIN, Ca-therine DORMOY, Pierre Emmanuel DROSTE, Éric DUFOUR, Herald DUPLESSY, Marie-France DUS-SAUSSOIS, Mounia EL GHARBOUJ, Sandra ELIAS-ZWICZ, Serge ELOIRE, Catherine EMONET, Pascal EUGENE, Vincent FALCUCCI, Valérie FAUGERAS, Dominique FELDSTEIN, Patricia FERARU, Nicolas FONTY, Danièle FORTE, FRIGO, Victor FUENTES, Fred GADAN, Francis GALLOIS-MONTBRUN, Christine GHIAI-FAR, François GILLET, Piotr GLE-GOLA, Édouard GRASSIN, Christophe GREA, Alain GRIGNET, Daniel GUETTA, Denis GUFFROY, Nico-las GUICHET, François GUIDON, Frédérique GUIL-LOUET, Damien HAMON, Brian HEMSWORTH, Karine HERMAN, Noé HERNANDEZ, Christiane HERVET, Thomas HEUZE, Anne-Marie HORS, Enrico INGALA, Youssef ISMAEL, Ariane JOUAN-NAIS, Laurent JOUANNEL, Claire KARSENTY, Laurent KARST, Pawel KORNECKI, Christophe KUNTZ, Christine LAEMLIN, Xavier LAGURGUE, Thierry LANDI, Hervé LANGLAIS, Clare LASBREY, Philippe LÊ, Jacques LE DU, Sophie LE PICARD, Élisabeth LEMERCIER, Hervé LEVASEUX, Pierre LEVAVASSEUR, Jacques LEVY-BENCHETON, David LONG, Alexis LORCH, Lionel LORIS, Babak MAD-DAH, Vincent MARCHAND, Bastien MARION, Renaud MARRET, Federico MASOTTO, Alberto MEDEM, Vincent MEGROT, Stanislas MELUN, Nicolas MEMI, Sophie MERTIAN, Christophe MICHEL, Maria-Grabiela MOLISE, Bach NGU-YEN, Sophie NICOLAS, Mojan NOUBAN, Camille NOURRIT, Malcolm NOUVEL, Cathy OLIVE, Jean-Marie PARANT, Éric PARISIS, Eddy PENOT, Ra-phaëlle PERRON, Véronique PETIT, Vitorio PISU, Sabine PLANCHOT, Hélène PLANEX, Michel PLA-XINE, Gérard PRAS, Anna PRICOUPENKO, Sophie PRUDHOMME, Astrid RAPPEL, Maya RAVEREAU, Jean-Jacques RAYNAUD, Nathalie REGNIER, Jean-François RENAUD, Lionel RENOUF, Jean-Michel REYNIER, Line SATTLER, Nathalie SCALI-RING-WALD, Toshio SEKIGUCHI, Arnaud SENESI, Gene-viève SHATER, Hayan SIDAOUI, Jérôme SIGWALT, N. SOUMAGNAC, Samy TALAOUBRID, Annemick THOMASSEN, Marie-Hélène TORCQ, Jean-Fran-çois TROULARD, Simone TROUVE, Isabelle VAS-SEUR, Philippe VASSEUR, Hélène VERNET, Matthieu VIEDERMAN, Elsa VINCENT-CORTESSE, Thomas VON AMELUNXEN, Claudia WENDER, George YIONTIS, Joanne YOUNG, Sylvaine ZABO-ROWSKI

Photography

Hervé ABADIE, Nicolas BOREL, Georges FESSY, Jean-Marie MONTHIERS, Thierry O'SUGHRUE

Models

ALPHA-VOLUMES, Éric CHICAEZ, Jean-Louis COURTOIS, Éric DELARUE, Olivier DOIZY, Jean-Michel FRANCOISE, Bruno ISAMBERT, Rod MARANI, David TOPANI

Art

Alberto BALI, Virginie CAMPION, Louis DERBRÉ, GATIMALAU, Vincent GONTHIER, François MORELLET, Anna PRICOUPENKO, François SEIGNEUR, Anton SOLOMOUKA

Landscape

David BESSON-GIRARD, Anne-Sylvie BRUEL, Christophe DELMAR, Kathryn GUSTAFSON, Karine HERMAN, Florence MERCIER, Philippe NIEZ, Michel PENA, Alfred PETER ROZOT, Alexandra SCHMIDT, Gilles VEXLARD

Consultants

Jean-Pierre AURY, Christian BARTENBACH, Georges BERNE, Jean-Louis BESNARD, Sophie BRINDEL-BETH, Daniel DAR-BOIS, J.P. DESCHAMPS, Pierre DIAZ-PEDREGAL, Jérôme DOURDIN Claude FUSÉE, Philippe LAIR, Marc MALINOWSKI, Pierre MIQUEL, Alain PAPI-NEAU, Richard PEDUZI, Sabine ROSANT, Jean-Paul ROYNETTE, Guillaume SAALBURG, Philippe UZZAN, Gérold ZIMMERLI

Perspectives

Jacques AILLAUD, Éric ANTON, Antoine BONO-MO, Anne et Denis CLEARY, Didier GHISLAIN, Philippe HARDEN, Douglas HARDING, Laurent HOCHBERG, Thierry LACOSTE, Vincent LAFONT, Louis PAILLARD, François ROBAIN, Jérôme SIG-WALT, Frédéric TERREAUX, Christophe VALTIN

Cooperating Practices

AR&C – Pierre Rigaudeau et Philippe Cœur, AVANT-TRAVAUX, Jean-Pierre BASTIDE, DELAGE et TSAROPOULOS, Gilles GAUVAIN, William GO-HIER, IVARS et BALLET, François JESTAZ, LAM-POTANG et SIEW, Éric LEGLEYE, Dominique PERRAULT, Jean-Paul ROUILLAT, Jean-Michel WIL-MOTTE

Illustration credits

Jean-Marie Monthiers Cover, 20, 30, 48, 52, 53, 54, 62, 75, 76, 77, 78, 93, 94, 95, 96, 97, 98, 105, 106, 107, 108, 109, 110, 113, 115, 116

Hervé Abadie 6, 14, 36, 60, 65, 67, 68, 119, 120, 121, 122

Dimension color 26

Nicolas Borel 18, 87, 88, 89, 90

Vincent Lafont 32

F. Achdou/Urba Images 34/35

Brunet/Saunier 38, 40, 42, 44, 46, 114

Georges Fessy 58, 72, 73, 81, 82, 83, 84, 101, 102

IGN 64, 70, 74, 80, 86, 92, 100, 104, 112, 118

Thierry O'Sughrue 66